C000184333

HILLSIDE GUIDES - ACROSS THE NORTH

The Uplands of Britain - full colour hardback books
- THE HIGH PEAKS OF ENGLAND & WALES
- YORKSHIRE DALES, MOORS & FELLS

Hillwalking - Lake District
- LAKELAND FELLS - SOUTH
- LAKELAND FELLS - EAST
- LAKELAND FELLS - NORTH
- LAKELAND FELLS - WEST

Long Distance Walks
- COAST TO COAST WALK   • DALES WAY   • CUMBRIA WAY
- WESTMORLAND WAY   • FURNESS WAY   • LADY ANNE'S WAY
- BRONTE WAY   • CALDERDALE WAY   • PENDLE WAY
- CALDERDALE WAY   • NIDDERDALE WAY   • TRANS-PENNINE WAY

Circular Walks - Yorkshire Dales
- WHARFEDALE   • MALHAMDALE   • SWALEDALE   • NIDDERDALE
- THREE PEAKS COUNTRY   • WENSLEYDALE   • HOWGILL FELLS

Circular Walks - Peak District
- NORTHERN PEAK   • CENTRAL PEAK   • EASTERN PEAK
- SOUTHERN PEAK   • WESTERN PEAK

Circular Walks - Lancashire
- BOWLAND   • PENDLE & THE RIBBLE   • WEST PENNINE MOORS

Circular Walks - North Pennines
- TEESDALE   • EDEN VALLEY   • ALSTON & ALLENDALE

Circular Walks - North York Moors
- WESTERN MOORS   • SOUTHERN MOORS

Circular Walks - South Pennines
- ILKLEY MOOR   • BRONTE COUNTRY
- CALDERDALE   • SOUTHERN PENNINES

WayMaster Visitor Guides
- YORKSHIRE DALES

---

*Send for a detailed current catalogue and price list
and also visit www.hillsidepublications.co.uk*

WALKING COUNTRY

CUMBRIA
WAY

Paul Hannon

Hillside

HILLSIDE
PUBLICATIONS
12 Broadlands
Shann Park
Keighley
West Yorkshire
BD20 6HX

First published 2005

© Paul Hannon 2005

ISBN 1 870141 76 8

Whilst the author has walked and researched all the route for the purposes of this guide, no responsibility can be accepted for any unforeseen circumstances encountered while following it. The publisher would appreciate information regarding material changes.

Cover illustration: Borrowdale and Derwentwater
Back cover: Coniston; Grange; River Brathay
Page One: Crinkle Crags from the Cumbria Way, Mickleden
Page Three: John Peel's grave, Caldbeck
Page Five: On the Cumbria Way in Great Langdale
(Paul Hannon/Hillslides Picture Library)

The sketch maps in this book are based upon
1947 Ordnance Survey One-Inch maps

Printed in Great Britain by
Carnmor Print
95-97 London Road
Preston
Lancashire
PR1 4BA

CONTENTS

THE CUMBRIA WAY

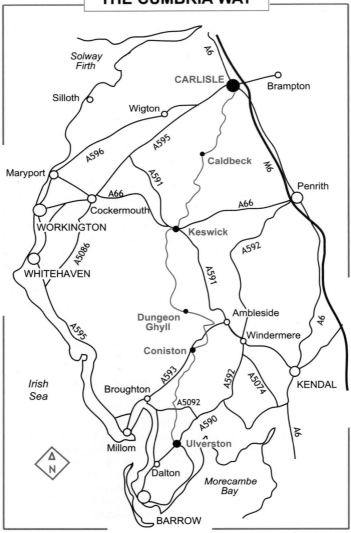

INTRODUCTION

The Cumbria Way is a 72-mile walk through the heart of the Lake District, commencing at Ulverston in the south and finishing at Carlisle in the north. Inspired by the rebirth of Cumbria as a county in 1974, the walk was pioneered by local groups of the Ramblers' Association, who did much to make the less known paths walkable. All but the first five miles and the final stage north of Caldbeck falls within the boundary of the Lake District National Park, the largest in England covering some 866 square miles.

For the most part the Cumbria Way remains on lower ground, crossing hills only twice in its entire length. The first is essential, as it negotiates the central watershed by way of the Stake Pass: this stage reveals the finest mountain scenery. Later, the Way pays belated respect to the hills by finally embracing the 2000ft contour on High Pike, northern outpost of the Lakeland Fells: even then, there is an easier alternative route for this part. The countryside through which the Way passes is of the highest order with beauty and grandeur at almost every turn, from lakeshores at Coniston and Derwentwater, to the valleys of Langdale and Borrowdale and the delightful smaller sheets of water such as Elterwater and Beacon Tarn. Make no mistake, the scenery is simply relentless!

The relatively easy walking and modest length of the Way mean that anyone taking a week off to walk it will find themselves with a day or two to spare. For this reason each stage concludes with an optional fellwalk, which you might enjoy by staying an extra night at some point and savouring a day on the hills without having your full rucksack with you. Whilst not the most demanding of walks, each takes you on a circuit around several summits, and they are of course better sampled on days of good weather.

Planning the walk

This guidebook has been divided into five logical stages, each offering a decent day's walking and ending at a suitable place to stay. There is a wide selection of accommodation along the Way, with campsites and youth hostels in amongst more up-market options. It is always wisest to book this in advance. The walk also has the advantage of both termini being accessible by rail: while Carlisle is on a main line, Ulverston is also just twenty minutes by train from Arnside, which also has a youth hostel.

In amongst the main route guide, notes of features along the way have been placed in *italics* to ensure that the essential route description is easy to locate. Often when reference is made to a gate there may also be a stile, but gates are more permanent and it saves some repetition.The sketch maps identify the location of the routes rather than the detail, and whilst the description should be sufficient to guide you around, a detailed map is recommended.

To gain the most from a walk, the detail of the Ordnance Survey 1:25,000 scale Explorer maps is unsurpassed. They also give an improved picture of your surroundings and the availability of linking paths. The following maps cover the route: • 315 Carlisle;

• OL4 - English Lakes North West;
• OL5 - English Lakes North East;
• OL6 - English Lakes South West;
• OL7 - English Lakes South East.

Additionally, mapmakers Harveys also produce an attractive Cumbria Way map. This has the advantage of covering the entire walk on one sheet, though its 1;40,000 scale does not show field boundaries.

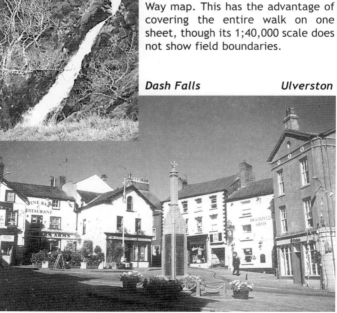

Dash Falls   *Ulverston*

FACILITIES

A general guide only

	Accommodation	Youth hostel	Campsite	Bus service	Rail station	Pub	Cafe/tearoom	Post office	other shop	WC	Phone box
Ulverston	•			•	•	•	•	•	•	•	•
Broughton Beck											•
Gawthwaite											•
Lowick	•			•		•					•
Torver	•		•	•		•					•
Bowmanstead	•		•	•		•					•
Coniston	•	•	•	•		•	•	•	•	•	•
Oxen Fell High Cross				•							
Little Langdale	•					•					•
Skelwith Bridge	•		•	•		•	•				•
Elterwater	•	•		•		•	•	•		•	•
Chapel Stile	•		•	•		•	•		•	•	•
Dungeon Ghyll	•		•	•		•	•				
Stonethwaite	•			•		•	•				
Rosthwaite	•	•		•		•	•		•	•	•
Grange	•		•	•		•	•			•	•
Portinscale	•		•	•		•	•		•		•
Keswick	•	•	•	•		•	•	•	•	•	•
Caldbeck	•			•		•	•	•	•	•	•
Hesket Newmarket	•			•		•	•	•			•
Sebergham				•							•
Bridge End				•		•			•		•
Dalston	•		•	•	•	•	•	•	•	•	•
Cummersdale				•		•					•
Carlisle	•	•		•	•	•	•	•	•	•	•

ULVERSTON TO CONISTON

DISTANCE 15¹⁄2 miles (25km)

ORDNANCE SURVEY MAPS
1:50,000
*Landranger 96 - Barrow in Furness & South Lakeland **or***
Landranger 97 - Kendal & Morecambe
1:25,000
Explorer OL6 - English Lakes South West

> *A delightful introduction to the Cumbria Way, beginning through undulating pastures and farms, and progressing to colourful open commons before a splendid lakeshore finish*

Ulverston is an unassuming market town on the southern fringes of Lakeland. Whilst not making claims to be a gateway to the Lakes, it nevertheless makes an ideal starting point for this route. A market charter was granted in 1280 by Edward I, and Thursday remains the traditional market day. Cobbled streets support numerous interesting shops; there is also a theatre and a heritage centre, and the Charter Festival takes place in September. St Mary's church dates back to the 12th century. Hartley's Brewery survives only as a depot for Robinsons, the Stockport company that acquired it in 1982 and ceased brewing nine years later. Nearby Swarthmoor Hall featured in the early Quaker movement, this Elizabethan manor house playing host to George Fox, founder of the Society of Friends.

Ulverston boasts several famous sons. Sir John Barrow, a much travelled explorer and founder member of the Royal Geographical Society, is remembered by a tall monument on Hoad Hill overlooking the town. Erected in 1850 in the style of Eddystone Lighthouse two years after his death, it makes a splendid short stroll, and needless to say is a fine viewpoint. Best known son is Stan Laurel, English half of that timeless comedy duo, Laurel and Hardy. Born here in 1890, the

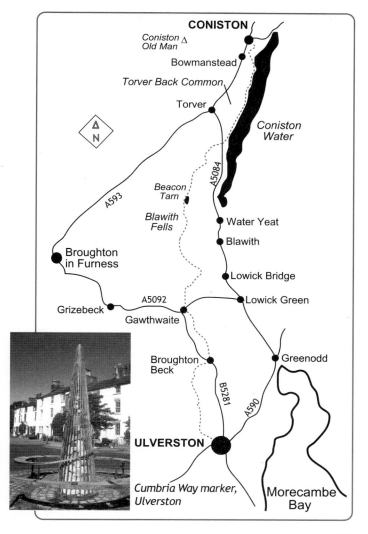

CONISTON

Coniston Old Man Δ

Bowmanstead

Torver Back Common

Torver

A5084

Coniston Water

Δ N

A593

Beacon Tarn

Blawith Fells

Water Yeat

Blawith

Lowick Bridge

Broughton in Furness

A5092

Lowick Green

Grizebeck

Gawthwaite

Broughton Beck

Greenodd

B5281

A590

ULVERSTON

Cumbria Way marker, Ulverston

Morecambe Bay

town's *Laurel & Hardy Museum is full of memorabilia. A hat-trick of worthies is completed by Lord Norman Birkett, who represented Britain at the post-World War Two Nuremburg Trials, and was also a valued conservationist.*

Long deemed inaccessible, Ulverston was usually approached by a treacherous cross-bay route, effectively a continuation of the better known Kent Sands route to the east. Things opened up in 1857 with the arrival of the railway, though continuation to Barrow lost Ulverston's advantage. Earlier, in 1796, the town's proximity to Morecambe Bay was exploited by the construction of a canal. Little more than a mile long, the Ulverston Canal was the widest and deepest in the country, and the sea lock at Canal Foot could accommodate very large craft. The waterway carried many commodities, notably locally worked iron and slate, and copper from Coniston, while bringing in items such as coal from Lancashire. Having been superceded by the railway it last saw commercial use early in the 20th century, and the lock gates were finally sealed in the 1940s.

The Cumbria Way leaves Ulverston at a car park at The Gill at the north-western edge of town. From the main thoroughfare of King Street go to its northern end in front of the Kings Arms Hotel, and turn left along Mill Street (past a historic 17th century mill which traded until 1970, refurbished as a pub in 2002) to find it. A modern sculpture of stones trapped within a metal frame incorporating seating, is the 'Cumbria Way marker', the official start point.

Head directly away from the sculpture at the tapering car park end, past some flower-draped cottages to the beginning of a surfaced pathway. This runs along the right side of the small stream of Town Beck into The Gill. Remain with it at a fork into wooded environs for a rapid departure from town to country. Shortly after a lone house across the stream, leave the main way (which the map confusingly also shows as the route) by a walled pathway to the left, crossing the head of The Gill and ascending steeply between wood and field. This winds up to a kissing-gate onto a back road, Stockbridge Lane. Don't join it however, but take a gap-stile on the right into the field, and head away with a wall on your left. *Across to the right is the Hoad Hill monument, while ahead can be seen the Old Man of Coniston far beyond the colourful western flank of little Flan Hill.* Remain with the wall through several fields, passing through intervening fence-stiles to the end corner where a gate admits onto a farm track. Advance along this to Old Hall Farm.

Take a gate on the right into the farmyard proper, and just beyond the house leave the drive by a stile on the left. After a few steps with a pleasant stream take another stile on the left immediately after the garden, and head diagonally across the field to a stile in the opposite wall at the end of Old Hall Wood. A thin path ascends outside the trees, slanting right to find a stile in the very top corner, reached by a few steps. Turn right along the field bottom, being deflected uphill by the enviably sited house and gardens at Bortree Stile. At the top corner a bridle-gate accesses a green track alongside the house.

Cross straight over to a twin gate and resume on a smashing little enclosed path ascending with a tiny stream. Towards the top a slate slab crosses it to a sturdy wall-stile into a field. Head directly away to quickly locate a ladder-stile ahead. This admits into a colourful tract of gorse-specked terrain, and an inviting grassy path rises away. *From here you can look back over the town to a wide panorama featuring Morecambe Bay, Bowland, Ingleborough and the Howgill Fells. Not for the last time will you espy the wind turbines on Kirkby Moor ahead, a major blot on the landscape for such insignificant benefit.*

At the top the path peters out to merge with a wall from the left, at which point cross it by a stile. *You now have massive views ahead to the Coniston Fells and Eastern Fells.* A thin path heads away towards the farm at Higher Lath, where a wall-stile admits onto the back road just in front. Turn right down the steeply winding road by colourful verges with further glorious views, most striking being the Coniston Fells featuring Dow Crag, the Old Man, Black Sails and Wetherlam.

Towards the bottom take a gate on the left immediately before the house at Windy Ash, and head along the wallside to the two dwellings at Newbiggin. A small gate leads you through the garden between them, onto the access road and directly away past the house at Newbiggin Farm. As the road swings sharp right, advance straight on a green way through a gate into the field ahead. Continue with a wall on the right through two fields, then across a field centre bound for the farmhouse at Stony Crag ahead. At a tree-lined stream bear left to find a fence-stile in a little corner and a simple crossing, to resume as before towards the house. A gate in front gives access to its yard, but turn immediately through another gate on the left.

Two grassy tracks head away: take the right one, up onto a minor brow behind the house', and on to a gate in front. Resume as before, along the fieldside with Hollowmire Farm ahead beneath another glimpse of Kirkby Moor wind turbines. Part way on, as a fence replaces the wall on your right, take a stile in it to cross the drain and resume on the other side of the hedge. This leads to the farm, going left on a narrowing way to a gate left of the house. Entering the yard, turn right behind the house and out on the access road. This runs to a T-junction with a through road.

Go left, enjoying a short stroll with fine views to the Coniston and High Street fells. As the road drops to a kink at a small open area, bear right to find a kissing-gate in the corner. Bound for the church in view, a thin path crosses the field to a gateway, and across the next towards the church. Pass left of the churchyard wall to a gate onto another road. *St John's church, Osmotherley (a parish rather than a place name) is a modest structure dating from 1873 and serving Broughton Beck and several farming hamlets.* Turn right past the church and along the road to a T-junction with the B5281 Ulverston-Gawthwaite road.

Go briefly left then right down the narrow road to Broughton Beck. As it swings right in the hamlet, continue straight down the no through road between a cluster of older buildings. This swings down to the left to continue as a cart track. This ends at a ford and slab footbridge. Don't cross, but take a gate on the left into a field. A track of sorts heads away to the right, towards tapering walls at the far corner. Don't pass through the fence crossing this narrow section, but take a wall-stile on the right and head directly away across the field. Attractive surrounds feature moorland to the left and undulating pastures ahead.

Approaching the stream of Broughton Beck go left to cross it at a stone slab bridge, then follow the beck upstream to a stile out of the field. A thin path now traces the beck to a further wall-stile where the stream parts company. Resume with a wall on your left, on through an old wall and on with a line of old trees on your left. At the end a wall takes over again, and the way traces an old, part-enclosed way along the fieldside to a corner stile cleverly utilising all three walls. Here a cart track is joined, and this leads on to join an unfenced road just ahead, beneath a gorse coloured slope under Lowick Beacon.

Go left along the road, becoming enclosed at a gate and on to the old farmhouse at Knapperthaw. Just past the house the road forks: bear right, quickly approaching another junction. This can be short-cut by a grassy track left across the open triangle. Then cross to a cattle-grid and gateway on the right sending a firm access road down across the field. *Ahead, the Helvellyn and Fairfield groups are now very distinct to the right of the Coniston Fells.* Entering woodland at a gateway, advance just 40 yards further then turn off left to find a couple of stiles into trees. From the right-hand one a path scales a short wooded bank to a stile into a sloping field bottom. Turn right, on above the house at Keldray to a wall-stile at the end. From it slant left up the bank to a stile part way up the facing wall, from where a wall leads away on a fieldtop. *More big views are enjoyed, particularly back over Morecambe Bay.* Towards the end you are ushered into the start of a walled cart track, which rises to Gawthwaite Farm on the edge of Gawthwaite. Simply advance through the gate and on along the short access road onto the A5092 Greenodd-Grizebeck road splitting the hamlet.

Cross to the green opposite, a splendid spot for a break by the small stream. *This also marks your entry, after just 5 miles, into the Lake District National Park, in which the Way will remain for the next 53 miles.* Directly ahead is the by-passed old road, and head off right on this narrow lane winding between colourful old cottages. This soon forks, the old road dropping down to meet the main one, while your way is the left fork. This rises away and runs on beneath an old slate quarry to a gate into colourful pasture. Though still classed as an old road, it becomes a little greener underfoot. *This is a glorious section beneath Gawthwaite Moor, with slabs of tilted rock up to the left, and grand views over the length of the Crake Valley, including a first cameo glimpse of Coniston Water.*

Advance through a gate at the end and on again to a gate at the next field end. Through this a footpath forks right through a gate to commence a slanting descent of a large pasture: part lined by gorse and still with super views, its grassing over surface suggests it once had greater status. At the bottom corner a gate sees it double sharply back down to the farm at High Stennerley. Pass to the right of the buildings to follow the access road away beneath the very attractive house, slanting down over a cattle-grid and above a wood to drop onto a back road. *At the end of summer the verges are rampant with a crop of blackberries.*

Go right briefly downhill, but well before the next farm, Kendall Ground (which started out under the auspices of Furness Abbey), take a gate on the left. Head across some unsavoury terrain with the field edge to your right, to find a gateway ahead. Pass through and bear right, running more pleasantly with an old boundary bank to a wall-stile at the end. A little path drops through trees onto another back road.

Go left on this, over a cattle-grid and enjoying a delightful few minutes as it weaves through immensely colourful terrain as far as a sharp bend right. Here bear left on the drive to Kiln Bank, dropping to bridge a stream, a cattle-grid then on up the field to approach the farm.

Immediately after the farm buildings turn right through a gate on an enclosed green way along the rear of the barns. A gate at the end admits onto the base of a pasture bedecked with small outcrops and scrub. Go left along the grassy wallside track, curving around to a fork. Take the right branch rising gently away over the minor brow. *Prominent on the skyline to the west is Black Combe's dark scalloped hollow.* The path swings more faintly right over Subberthwaite Bank to be greeted by a grand scene ahead with the cluster of buildings at Tottlebank beneath the waiting Tottlebank Height. The way now runs more clearly on to a gate onto open common. An inviting green track heads away through the bracken, swinging left to soon rise to meet the access road to Tottlebank. Continue left on this, climbing to level out to approach the houses.

Just forty yards short of the surfaced road end (at the first house drive), double back right on a green path up the encroaching bracken slope. This quickly levels out to begin a delectable traverse along the eastern flank of Tottlebank Height, giving super views north and east beyond a seemingly profound drop towards the Crake Valley. The path soon begins an equally fine descent towards the lone house at Cockenskell (Cockenshell on older maps), meeting another path from the right at the foot of the hill. Go forward on this alongside a wall, and in a corner where the path goes left to remain on the common, instead take a gate in front. Advance with the wall on your left, through the field to quickly become enclosed by walls. The house at Cockenskell is across to the right. This green way drops down to a gate overlooking a small stream in conifer trees.

Ignore the path right and drop down the little path in front, into the trees and quickly swinging right, upstream to cross on a grassy stone bridge. The stile behind admits onto more common, a corner of the Blawith Fells. An inviting green path climbs away through bracken, quickly forking. The main right one rises to another early fork, this time go left to continue gently uphill, absorbing the earlier left branch. Together they ascend the bracken-draped fellside, briefly flirting with a wall on passing above a small plantation corner, then a little more steeply before quickly levelling out beneath Wool Knott to the left.

Suddenly Beacon Tarn is revealed ahead, a blue gem backed by the shapely, more distant Dow Crag. Remain on the path descending gently to arrive at the southern tip of the tarn, alongside its tiny outflow.

The main route of the Way crosses the outflow and follows the west bank of the tarn, absorbing a path from Wool Knott and staying close to the bank to the far end. *More rewarding is the marginally harder eastern shore path, undulating over colourful craggy knolls to rejoin the Way just beyond the tarn.* At 836ft/255m the Beacon rises modestly up above. Just a very slight rise follows to a saddle, which at some 625ft/190m is the surprisingly low 'high point' of the day.

From the brow the rougher continuing path drops down above a dead-flat moss. At the end of this the second half of the descent is made on a super path raking right down through bracken to the edge of the larger Stable Harvey Moss. On levelling out to arrive at a fork, bear left beneath a small outcrop, curving round the low spur leading to a crossroads of paths. Go right, crossing the moss's outflow stream, Black Beck, by stepping-stones just below. Mounting another minor brow, a green path quickly meets an unfenced access road.

Beacon Tarn, Blawith Fells,
looking north to Dow Crag and Coniston Old Man

Advance left up this a short way, and well before the wall ahead go left on a bridleway. This grassy track heads away along the edge of the moss. At a fork either left (level) or right (upper) can be taken, as they soon merge. The way then runs on with parallel overhead wires, and with Torver Tarn ('disused reservoir' on map) in view just ahead. The track swings right away from the poles and becomes less obvious. Approaching a tiny stream and then the slightly livelier Mere Beck fork left, passing under the lines and curving right to cross the sluggish upper stream. The overhead lines are re-crossed and a better green way heads off through bracken. This quickly runs to another stream, the outflow from the reservoir. Just across this is a cross-paths where you should turn right, but for now advance the few steps further to the old dam on Torver Low Common. *Locally known as Torver Tarn, this splendidly colourful spot is backed by the Old Man of Coniston.*

Return to the cross-paths and turn left on an initially less obvious path down through the bracken, descending in company with the chirpy, scrub-lined stream. This soon levels out in a colourful basin in this super side valley, and a grand path leads ultimately to a confluence with Torver Beck. This sizeable beck is crossed by a sturdy footbridge which superceded stepping-stones just downstream by the confluence. On the other side the path rises by a wall to a kissing-gate onto the A5084 Lowick-Torver road.

Cross straight over to a parking area and turn right on a cart track. This winds up onto Torver Back Common and along to a gate where Coniston Water makes its first real appearance. Remain on the main path slanting down to the wall below, and quickly working its way down to the lakeshore alongside a little jetty. *This is a seasonal landing stage for the Coniston launch, the stylish way to Coniston.* With the day's navigational duties largely over, simply turn left on the lakeshore path for Coniston. Though not always exactly on the shore, it's never more than a few yards away as the clear path runs through bracken, scrub and sections of scattered woodland along the base of the common. In time Torver Common Wood is entered, and after forking right in denser woodland the Way eventually reaches another landing stage.

Coniston Water is fourth largest of the English lakes, and until 1974 was the major lake of Lancashire. A string of famous names have had connections with the lake. Three, in chronological order, are John Ruskin, Arthur Ransome and Donald Campbell. Ruskin, Victorian artist, poet, critic and environmentalist, spent the last thirty years of his life at Brantwood, overlooking the lake, until his death in 1900. Open to visitors, it features a fine collection of his drawings and watercolours, furniture and possessions, along with a gallery, bookshop, tearoom and delightful gardens. Ransome was an author best known for children's adventures in his 'Swallows and Amazons' books, set on and around the lake. Campbell was the water speed record-breaker who tragically perished while attempting to beat his own record here in 1967. The Sun Hotel, in the village, contains mementoes of his time here.

A pleasing sight on the lake is the Victorian steam yacht Gondola. After near eighty years service it ceased operating in 1937, but painstaking restoration by the National Trust saw this elegant craft resume its role in 1980. Today you can you enjoy an opulent lake cruise, perhaps stopping off at Brantwood. Joining it is a separate enterprise the Coniston Launch, which operates as a seasonal ferry service around the lake, calling at various jetties including Brantwood.

The lakeshore path continues, soon reaching a boating centre. A gate here finally signals the exit from Torver Back Common access land. *Though now very difficult to locate, a large number of bloomeries were strung along this western shoreline, small iron furnaces of which many were run by the monks of Furness Abbey. The mined ore was smelted with charcoal to produce iron, indeed such was this demand for charcoal that much of the district's woodland was lost.* Advance on the track heading away, but after a second gate quickly bear right to a concession path through a kissing-gate. This keeps you close by the shore in the environs of a camping site. After a footbridge the site is left at twin gates, and a firm lakeshore path continues.

Brantwood can be seen amid trees on the eastern shore of the lake, while to the left are the rugged eastern aspects of the Coniston Fells featuring the Old Man, Brim Fell, Swirl How and Wetherlam. Through a gate at the end a continuing broader track leaves the lake, becoming a hard access road serving the Coniston Hall campsite you are now entering. Remain on this to approach the buildings, then bear right to the Hall itself. *Coniston Hall is the area's most interesting building, a late 16th century manor house with great round chimneys. It passed to the National Trust in 1972, and has a seasonal campsite shop.*

Pass left of the house and follow the access road out past a large sailing club. From a gate between two barns the road goes off left: advance straight on the firm path across the field, with Coniston village just ahead. From a gate at the end the path swings left to a sharp bend.

At one time the official route of the Way broke off faintly left here to a kissing-gate below a clump of trees, on again to a stile and up the field to a stile onto the A5084 at Bowmanstead, an outlying hamlet of Coniston boasting a pub, the Ship. The main route bears right on the hard path, to a gate and along another fieldside to emerge via a stile onto a sharp bend of Lake Road. Go left on the footway to enter the village centre. The true centre is just to the right, across the bridge on Church Beck.

Coniston is a bustling village with classic Lakeland attributes: as a result, vast crowds of summer visitors throng the few streets and the lakeshore. It boasts an idyllic setting sandwiched between its own lake and its own mountain. The attractive slate buildings shelter beneath towering fells crowned by the Old Man of Coniston himself, from whose slopes much of the slate was won. Coniston is perhaps better known as having been Lakeland's principal copper mining area, the major sites being in Coppermines Valley a mile above the village in the lap of the Old Man: the industry peaked in the mid-19th century, when it employed over 500 men. A branch railway arrived in 1859 from Foxfield to transport copper and slate from the mines and quarries, but closed, inevitably, in 1957.

Coniston Hall

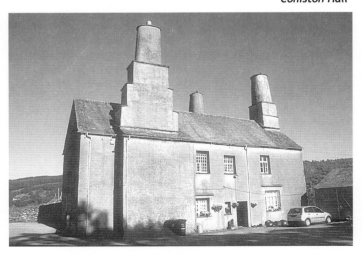

The village's facilities include a Post office, various shops, four pubs and two youth hostels. St Andrew's church dates from 1819, and in the churchyard a large Anglo-Saxon type cross commemorates John Ruskin, who died here in 1900 and had opted for Coniston churchyard over Westminster Abbey. A museum was opened in the village shortly after his death, and remains a good all-weather attraction for visitors as it tells a comprehensive Coniston story. The Campbell memorial takes the form of a T-shaped seat on the little green, while a National Park Centre stands nearby. A welcome addition to the Coniston scene was the opening of a small brewery at the rear of the Black Bull in 1995, and its award winning products can be tasted within.

A FELLWALK FROM CONISTON

DISTANCE *8 miles/13km*   ASCENT *2900ft/885m*

SUMMITS
Coniston Old Man   2634ft/803m   *Brim Fell   2611ft/796m*
Swirl How   2631ft/802m

ORDNANCE SURVEY MAPS
1:50,000 - Landranger 96
1:25,000 - Explorer OL6

The Old Man of Coniston is one of Lakeland's favourite characters. The lower slopes bear fascinating evidences of copper mining activity, absorbing industrial relics overshadowed by high level slate quarries. Such is the mountain's resilience that it shrugs off such blemishes to still project an endearing front. Leave the village centre by a narrow road on the south side of the bridge on Church Beck. This climbs to the Sun Hotel immediately behind which a narrow, short-lived lane runs on to end at a gate at the last buildings. *Already a great skyline hovers ahead, featuring Great How Crags on Swirl How.* A broad track runs through the field, crossing a sidestream just above its confluence with Church Beck, then climbing above the wooded main beck. The going eases and the track runs past fine waterfalls to Miners Bridge. A path continues upstream, soon reaching a gate in a descending wall. *This superb moment reveals an imposing skyline running from Coniston Old Man's summit towards Swirl How. In front is Coppermines Valley with the white-walled youth hostel prominent, above which are waterfalls on both Low Water Beck and Levers Water Beck.*

The path makes gentle progress above the valley, rising to a wall corner at the top then on to the last wall, just behind. Quarry spoil beneath you is just one example of the remains that will be seen. Continuing, the path rises onto an old quarry road. Turn right up this a matter of yards to a fork. Take the left-hand one which spirals steeply up to arrive at an extensive former quarry site. *Looking back, Coniston Water is fully revealed.* Pass through two level sections of ruins of stone sheds, with rusting cables and tramway tracks in amongst the spoil heaps. Continue up to a fork, with a dark tunnel just to the left beneath a prostrate cable stanchion. Bear right, quickly rising past the main quarry face and away from the site. A few minutes further, the path arrives at the basin of Low Water. This is a stunningly located mountain tarn, with the summit ridge brooding directly above. A path runs the few extra yards to the bouldery shore.

The final stage of the climb sees the path rising left, engaging a fine series of zigzags up to yet more quarry evidence. These smaller workings are negotiated on part restored paths to reach more open ground. The path then treads easier terrain for the final few minutes to the immense slate platform marking the Old Man's summit. *Perched above the steep eastern face, it offers a classic bird's-eye view into Low Water. If looking elsewhere one cannot fail to be impressed by the two-sided picture. Inland rise the hills, with neighbouring Dow Crag magnificent and the Scafell group equally impressive beyond. The southern arc, meanwhile, depicts the decreasing foothills of South Lakeland, intermingled with lakes and tarns and culminating in an extensive coastline formed by the various indentations of Morecambe Bay.*

From the Old Man long strides are the order of the day, turning northwards along the rim of Low Water's combe, with a broad path on excellent turf leading to the solid cairn on Brim Fell. *Little more than a stepping-stone between the two major tops, Brim Fell also holds the dubious distinction of being the least interesting summit in this group of hills. A visit to the eastern slopes is repaid with a striking view down into the heart of the copper mining district; here its rugged east face can be seen to conform to the general pattern of the group.*

Along the whaleback ridge the saddle of Levers Hause interrupts the climb to Swirl How. *From this vicinity there are good views down over Levers Water to Coniston village and lake.* The short climb to the summit of Swirl How is interrupted by the modest tops of Little How Crags and Great How Crags, still with excellent views down to the right. Swirl How's almighty summit cairn appears just two minutes before reaching it across a tilted, stony plateau. *Reaching seven feet into the sky, it hovers above an unbroken plunge to the Greenburn Valley. This is a grand place to be, for Swirl How is undeniably the kingpin of the Coniston Fells, with ridges radiating to all points of the compass.*

Within yards of the cairn to the east, a splendid descent of the east ridge commences by way of Prison Band: though a heady mountain atmosphere pervades, nothing more than an occasional rock step is encountered. *Ahead meanwhile is isolated Wetherlam, which initially appears subdued but gains in stature as height is lost.* At the base of the ridge the neat, intervening col of Swirl Hause is reached. While the main path continues east to cross the flank of Black Sails to Wetherlam, your path swings off right, bound for the waiting Levers Water. The path runs down to its shore at a very undemanding gradient, indeed the opening section is merely a traverse across Black Sails' flank, well above Swirl Hause Beck. Surprisingly the path loses its way a little lower down, but the line is distinct enough to gain the rocky shoreline. Go left on a clearer path to the outflow, and descend a stony track. Initially very rough, it soon improves to pass beneath the brooding Kennel Crag up to the left.

With the Paddy End Copper Works site below, the track reaches a hairpin bend. Go straight ahead on a contrastingly inviting green path, slanting down the bracken fellside and across a leat: *this is one of a series built to convey water from the becks to the mines to help power machinery.* Coniston Coppermines appear below, and at a fork the main branch curves down to the right onto the old mine road, thence going left down to the hostel and associated restored buildings.

Conclude by heading off down the long, level mine road through the Coppermines Valley. Simply remain on this to finish, passing en route the Miners Bridge which could of course be crossed if desired. Otherwise, the rough road drops down by some extremely lively scenery, as Church Beck tumbles in fine waterfalls down through a deep gorge. On acquiring a surface the road runs back to the village centre alongside the Black Bull.

2

CONISTON TO DUNGEON GHYLL

DISTANCE 12¹⁄₂ miles (20km)

ORDNANCE SURVEY MAPS
1:50,000
Landranger 96 - Barrow in Furness & South Lakeland or
Landranger 97 - Kendal & Morecambe
and
Landranger 90 - Penrith, Keswick & Ambleside
1:25,000
Explorer OL6 - English Lakes South West
Explorer OL7 - English Lakes South East

> *Mostly gentle walking on well used paths, this leisurely amble through the heart of central Lakeland's 'low country' offers a classic Langdale pub crawl in its second half*

Leave the village centre by turning down the road past the church, keeping right past the Crown Hotel and along to a junction with a road signed left to Ambleside. Turn along this, passing a sports centre and along a little further until level with the school. Here turn right over stone-arched Shepherd Bridge on Yewdale Beck, then immediately left over a stile for a few yards upstream. A kissing-gate leads into a big sloping field, where the improving path rises away. A short line of trees lead on to a corner, continuing to a kissing-gate at the tapering field end alongside an intriguing building. *This is a restored Gothic folly built for foxhounds by the Marshall family who acquired the Monk Coniston estate in 1835. A century later it was bought by the children's author Beatrix Potter, and passed to the National Trust. Since restored it now serves as a shelter with wooden benches.*

The path rises behind the folly up a part wooded knoll, then up to a gate in a wall, and continues rising to a fork. Ignore the right branch crossing to the wall, but continue up the inviting direct path to pass between dense gorse. *Here pause to look back to a fine prospect of the Coniston triumvirate: lake, village and Old Man.* From a kissing-gate in the wall ahead, the path runs through the short-lived Back Guards Plantation, emerging via a gate at the other side into more agreeable open surrounds. The pleasant path heads away, with a superb view left to the craggy front of the Yewdale Fells. Steadily declining through a long pasture, the path fades. Keep towards the right side until at the end bear left a little to a gate ahead. Head through this field centre to find a gate at the far end onto a walled bridle-track. Go left on this rough lane, dropping to rejoin the crystal-clear Yewdale Beck which leads upstream to a sturdy bridge at Low Yewdale.

Don't cross the bridge, but take the stile in front and head away around the hedgeside of the big flat field. From a stile at the end the beck is briefly rejoined in woodland. After a short way the path swings off to the right, commencing an enjoyable pull through Tarn Hows

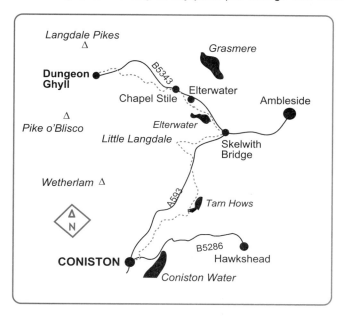

25

Wood. Rising to meet a broader track in front of a deer fence, pass through the gate and continue climbing through conifers. A similar gate at the top leads back out into better woodland. The way rises left, meeting a woodland boundary wall and becoming a nicer path. Remain in the wood as the path ascends with the wall, giving glorious views out across the Yewdale scene. Levelling out to leave by a small gate at the top corner, a short little path then runs on to reach Tarn Hows Cottage in an idyllic setting.

Turn right through a gate and climb away on its access road, which levels out to wind round with fine views north to Helvellyn and Fairfield. On meeting a narrow road on the open common of Tarn Hows Intake, turn left. *This affords continually outstanding views to rugged Wetherlam overlooking the richly wooded old quarrying area of Tilberthwaite.* Remain on the road for a steep rise to approach Tarn Hows and the highest point of the day, again a modest one at around 690ft/210m. On the right is a large car park, and just at its end, a path turns off left onto the open grass overlooking the tarn.

This is a splendid moment as you appraise one of Lakeland's most popular 'chocolate box' scenes. A clue that this is a major tourist venue is given by a sign warning of the perils of '..slipping on the grass'. Originally an area of marsh and pools known as The Tarns, it was dammed over a century ago by the Marshalls of Monk Coniston Hall to power a sawmill and the whole area was ambitiously landscaped. Beatrix Potter's acquisition of the entire estate in 1929 saw it passed on to the National Trust. The grassy slopes overlooking the tarn enable it to be viewed as a foreground to a fine mountain backdrop, in which the Langdale Pikes make their first appearance of the day.

Resume by taking the main path left down to the foot of the tarn, then running on into the trees. It soon leaves the shore, but remains in pleasant surrounds still with glimpses through the trees (much closer to the tarn than the map suggests). At a fork keep right on the main path nearer the shore. Nearing the end of the tarn, and very close to the shore, the path forks: here leave the circuit path on a very clear path left, signed to 'Arnside and Langdales'. This runs on through splendid open country to arrive at a gate onto an old walled lane. Turn left on this cart track, which remains underfoot for a considerable time, soon opening out with good views and ultimately merging into a narrow back road. Continue down this to meet the A593 Coniston-Ambleside road by a cottage at Oxen Fell High Cross.

Cross with care to a minor road opposite, but instead of following it, turn right on a path though the trees. Quickly emerging at a kissing-gate it continues to parallel the main road over the wall, rejoining it at another kissing-gate. You need not set foot on it, however, as a path goes immediately left through bracken to a junction of minor access roads leaving the main road at Tong Intake. *An information panel tells something of this area's slate-quarrying history which lasted to the mid-20th century.*

Bear right on the road outside the walled wood, this very pleasant cul-de-sac way runs for some time through scenery very typical of this corner of Lakeland. Ultimately rising to a brow it presents an inspiring new scene, with Little Langdale being the foreground to a mountain skyline including Helvellyn, Fairfield, Red Screes and Ill Bell. The road swings down to the enviably sited High Park, with its backdrop of Little Langdale under Lingmoor Fell and beyond to Crinkle Crags and Bowfell.

The Cumbria Way at High Park, Little Langdale, looking to Bowfell

Here leave the road by dropping down the short drive to the buildings, then go immediately right through a kissing-gate and a path rakes across the field to another gate in a wall. Go left along the top side of the wall to reach a gate into the wood, and within yards is a major fork. The true Cumbria Way runs straight on the wallside bridleway. The far superior route is the well-worn permissive path dropping left through the trees. It descends considerably to the bank of the Brathay, then just a little further downstream arrives at Colwith Force. *Though popular enough it is still one of Lakeland's less celebrated waterfalls, but it is a magnificent spectacle.*

A short path breaks off left onto a knoll where great caution is urged as you witness the upper falls and peer down onto the main fall. Back on the main path, it runs high above the beck before dropping down to another junction, where a short path doubles back left to a more conventional viewpoint for the main falls. Resume downstream on a firmer path above the beck as it runs through trees to drop down to a choice of stiles onto the road at Colwith Bridge.

Turn right very briefly then take a stile on the left. A path crosses the small pasture to rejoin the Brathay, but at a stile into woodland it climbs the wooded bank to a stile at the top. While the beck departs to head for Elterwater, the path crosses a field to a house ahead. *Before entering the grounds turn to look back over a wonderful scene dominated by Wetherlam, with Wet Side Edge rising above Greenburn to Great Carrs, and the Wrynose Pass leading around to Pike o'Blisco.*

Through an iron kissing-gate cross straight over the drive, and through a small gate a briefly enclosed path heads away. From a stile at the end cross a tiny stream and on to a stile in the wall ahead, then on to the driveway at the cluster of buildings at Elterwater Park (Park Farm on the map). *Note the slate alphabet on the wall on the right.* Go straight along the front of the house, and through a gate at the end. From here an initially enclosed track winds down the slope, down to a gate and stream crossing at the bottom and then on to the far end. Kissing-gates and a bridge lead onto another drive at Park House.

Again go straight ahead, following the drive out: here be sure to look back left for a smashing prospect of the Langdale Pikes. When the drive swings right towards the road, keep straight on the clear path running towards woodland. A kissing-gate admits into Bridge How Coppice, and the broad path descends steeply, runs on over a stream and to a kissing-gate back out of the trees. The path continues past a bungalow to a kissing-gate onto its drive, just yards short of the A593 again. Go left with care for the couple of minutes it takes to drop around to Skelwith Bridge. *Across the road stands a boundary marker indicating the 'County Palatine of Lancashire'. This refers to the fact that until 1974 administrative changes, the entire Cumbria Way to this point was within Lancashire. On crossing the bridge you enter old Westmorland, while Cumberland will take over on the Stake Pass.*

Across the double-arched bridge on the Brathay turn immediately left upstream. To your right is the imposing Skelwith Bridge Hotel. *This overlooks the meeting of the A593 Ambleside-Coniston road and the B5343 Great Langdale road. Just around the back is the hotel's public bar, known as the Talbot.* Ahead meanwhile is a giftshop and cafe, pass to their right on the narrow access road leading to the working slate yard, and keep on a path at the end into trees. This runs a tight course between the Brathay and the road, quickly arriving above Skelwith Force, which demands a few yards' detour. *The lack of height is more than compensated for by its ferocity, as a substantial volume of water is forced through a narrow rock passage: nevertheless, it is not in the same league as Colwith Force.*

The upper section of Colwith Force

Resume on the path above the lively river to reach a gate out of the trees. In these new open surrounds the Brathay opts for a quieter life, and a splendid stride on a firm path shadows the river (not as per map) to soon arrive at the foot of Elterwater. *A bench occupies this delectable spot, a moment to halt as you are presented with a neatly framed view of the Langdale Pikes beyond the reed-fringed shoreline. Savour your only moment in the lake's company. This charming mere is classed as the smallest of the 17 lakes (as opposed to Lakeland's many scores of tarns). Elterwater collects the waters of Great Langdale Beck (from Great Langdale) and the River Brathay (from Little Langdale), releasing them as the latter. It was named by the Norsemen, meaning 'swan lake', and these elegant birds can still be found on it.*

Remain on the path which passes through a gate into woodland to lose the lake's presence, running on through trees to emerge with Great Langdale Beck, a popular beckside route (not as per map) all the way to the car park in Elterwater village. Advance to the entrance by the bridge. While the Way turns left over the bridge, few if any will give Elterwater such short shrift. *Elterwater is a hugely popular little Lakeland village, its tiny sloping green and white-walled pub, the Britannia, being a guaranteed magnet. The village Post office/shop also faces onto the green, with a WC and bowling green alongside. A popular youth hostel is just a hundred yards along the road, while a bracken-covered common to the north lends itself to relaxing picnics.*

From the green return to the bridge, across which turn right up a road which serves a slate quarry. Shortly after levelling out, a massive, gated quarry hole is reached on the left. With the working quarry just ahead, the footpath is signed to the right, slanting down to Great Langdale Beck. Follow this upstream through the trees. *Camouflaged in the trees opposite is the initially controversial Langdale timeshare complex, built in the early 1980s on the site of a gunpowder factory.* A loop of the beck is by-passed, then it returns to lead beneath old quarry spoil heaps to a footbridge. Cross to emerge onto the road on the edge of Chapel Stile. Turn left past the Wainwrights Inn. *Formerly the White Lion, its sign depicts the craft of cart making, rather than the legendary guidebook writer!*

Much of this village originated to provide accommodation for workers in the slate quarries. The Holy Trinity church looks down from a natural platform, a perfect advertisement for the local material as it blends harmoniously into the steep fellside. Just a little further is the village centre with shop and cafe. The route, however, turns left opposite the WC, on a firm track up a tract of open ground. It runs on past the rear of the school to another small open tract. Bear left on the access road, but then at once keep right as a fork goes left. This soon expires at the cottages of Thrang Farm, where bear right to a small gate. *Ahead is a first truly stunning picture of the Langdale Pikes.*

Through the gate a short-lived footway runs between walls to join an access road, with the valley road just to your right on the edge of the village. However, turn left on this farm road to quickly wind round beneath quarry spoil to cross the beck by the slate arched New Bridge. The rough road turns upstream to run a smashing course parallel with the remarkably clear beck, largely with a grassy flood embankment to hand. *The prize feature of this stage, quite obviously, is the prospect of the Langdale Pikes straight along the flat valley floor.* Ignoring a drive branching off to Baysbrown Farm, keep straight on until alongside a bridge the track bears left to the idyllically sited house at Oak Howe.

Pass along the front to a path junction in front of a fine barn. Here turn right past the barn to continue up-dale on what quickly becomes a delightful green path between old walls. Emerging, the path runs on to a gate to forge on along the base of Lingmoor Fell, keeping above the intake wall with the deep channelled Great Langdale Beck below. *Dungeon Ghyll appears with the Langdale Pikes rising protectively behind, a classic picture. Note, for the record, that the placename*

The Britannia, Elterwater

Dungeon Ghyll does not appear on OS maps, simply New Hotel and Old Hotel. Though less dramatic than the Pikes, the big dalehead skyline peaks of Bowfell and Crinkle Crags are now in view, the former being some 500ft superior to the Pikes. Crossing a stream to a sheepfold, a gate at the end sees a rebuilt path strike down a large pasture to a gate, then alongside the wall to Side House. *For a direct route to the campsite ignore the route into Side House and Dungeon Ghyll, and instead bear left up above the house to a ladder-stile, from where a permissive path runs through the fields to drop down into the site.*

Cross a simple footbridge and turn into the yard, then follow the short drive out over Great Langdale Beck to join the main valley road, the B5343. Go left a few paces and turn into the National Trust's large Stickle Gill car park. At the top end you have the option to go right for refreshment. *Dungeon Ghyll is the heart of the Langdale scene: the New Hotel stands at the very foot of Stickle Gill, descending from Stickle Tarn. Alongside is another pub, the Stickle Barn Tavern. Dungeon Ghyll itself is the next beck to the west, which carves its own ravine down from the celebrated Langdale Pikes which tower above. The famous climbers' base of the Old Hotel is located a long half-mile further along the valley - soon be there now!*

From the information shelter at the top of the car park, a path rises between two small pockets of trees, through a gate into a small enclosure behind. Continue up, joined by the path from the hotel to rise between two further small clusters of trees and then fork immediately left from the restored path by Stickle Gill, on a path rising to a gate on the brow. Again fork immediately left to run alongside the wall along the base of the fell. It drops to a wooden footbridge on Dungeon Ghyll itself and resumes in splendid style beneath the craggy fellside.

Throughout this final stage the views are simply staggering: this is superlative mountain country. Directly across the valley is Pike o'Blisco, and moving round to the dalehead are the loftier Crinkle Crags and Bowfell. Continue in this fashion to become part enclosed, and along to a gate to the rear of the Dungeon Ghyll Old Hotel, where double back left down to its car park. *Though the through route forges straight on, it is unimaginable that anyone might not turn aside at the 'Old DG'. The public bar with its stone flagged floors is an unchanging Lakeland refuge, home to steaming waterproofs and superb beer. Pretty much everything you see hereabouts is in the care of the National Trust, from the hotel and campsite to the rugged felltops.*

The Langdale Pikes from Chapel Stile

A FELLWALK FROM DUNGEON GHYLL

DISTANCE 7 miles/11km   *ASCENT* 2950ft/900m

SUMMITS
Sergeant Man   2411ft/735m   High Raise   2500ft/762m
Thunacar Knott   2372ft/723m   Pavey Ark   2296ft/700m
Harrison Stickle 2415ft/736m   Pike o'Stickle   2326ft/709m
Loft Crag   2238ft/682m

ORDNANCE SURVEY MAPS
1:50,000 - Landranger 89 & Landranger 90
1:25,000 - Explorer OL6

This full circuit of the Langdale Pikes includes High Raise, overlord of the group. Though hidden by the bold front of the Pikes and exerting little influence on them, it is the major mountain at the epicentre of Lakeland and makes a more complete round of these fells. Start from the New Hotel, Dungeon Ghyll.

From the hotel drive, go straight on through a gate by the side of a cottage. Head up the wallside to a gateway and into an enclosure behind. Rise between clusters of trees and remain on the restored path by Stickle Gill. The lively beck is soon crossed at a footbridge to resume upstream, passing through the centre of an old sheepfold. At the next sidestream, don't cross but take a clear path doubling back up to the right. This too has been repaired, and provides a splendid zigzag ascent. Half way up the path forks, the left branch crossing the stream before climbing to the base of Tarn Crag. Ignore this, and instead retain the traditional grassy zigzags. The fine peak of Harrison Stickle soars across Stickle Gill. The path remains a gem all the way up to the side of a crumbling enclosure. *Improving views look back over the valley to the Coniston Fells and around to Crinkle Crags at the dalehead.*

Passing a ruin on the left, the zigzags fade on a grassy tongue. Higher again, the fading path slants left away from the gill, but can be followed above a lesser sidestream onto easier ground. Though very faint now, all is made clear as the rocky dome of Sergeant Man appears. Dramatically and suddenly it is followed by the awesome cliff of Pavey Ark straight in front, and within seconds Harrison Stickle joins it to form a superlative pairing. Advance in the direction of Sergeant Man to join a clear, level path. At the same time Stickle Tarn appears over to the left.

Turn right on this path away from the drama for a short, level tramp. Starting to climb through a stony area, cairns quickly indicate a fork. Bear left, passing a ruined shelter. The path becomes faint here, and soon turns to rise up the inviting grassy slopes between low rock outcrops. One or two cairns aid progress, and the path quickly gains the ridge descending from Sergeant Man, dividing Langdale from Easedale. If the ascent path is lost, the better one along the broad ridge is more easily found.

First look back at the classic view of Stickle Tarn and its guardian peaks, then ahead to the long skyline of the Fairfield Horseshoe and the Ill Bell ridge. The still thin path meanders pleasantly left, and at one of its cairns the craggy summit dome of Sergeant Man re-appears. The path works round to a better defined dip in the ridge at a small pool: at this point the Helvellyn massif appears to the north. Just a few yards across the ridge, cairns confirm the presence of the main ridge path. Just ahead, the well worn Easedale path also gains the ridge from the other side.

The next ten minutes present a choice of paths. The Easedale one is promoted by cairns guiding onto it, while a thinner one keeps to the Langdale side. Either way, both climb the ridge, passing modest outcrops and merging near a tilted slab. Continuing, the summit peak of Sergeant Man beckons more closely, and is soon revealed for what it really is - a marvellous sham - as near-level ground is seen running away behind it. The path curves around to gain a neat cairn on the rocky top. *This is a grand place to be, looking down over Bright Beck to the arresting profile of Pavey Ark above Stickle Tarn.*

Least interesting part of the view is north-west to High Raise, and this is the direction to take. Of several paths radiating away, the main one crosses rougher ground before a gentle rise to the summit. En route it merges with a line of forlorn fenceposts, and 200 yards short of the top these turn off to the right. The path keeps straight on to gain the OS column and shelter on a rash of stones, from where the fell derives its older name of High White Stones. *Being the very hub of the district, High Raise commands a first-rate panorama. There is interest in all points of the compass, from nearby Crinkle Crags, Bowfell, Esk Pike and Scafell Pike, round to Great Gable, Pillar, High Stile and Grasmoor. Northwards are the giants of Skiddaw and Blencathra, while the long Helvellyn range is unbroken to the east. Of particular note however are more individual features such as the view up Borrowdale and the arresting profile of Honister Crag to the north-west.*

Leave on the path heading south, bound for the Langdale Pikes. *Currently they are overtopped by the Coniston Fells, while to the right is majestic Bowfell.* A long steady decline leads to a saddle at the head of Bright Beck. Continue straight up the facing slope, ignoring a broad branch left, and onto the domed top of Thunacar Knott. A sturdy cairn to the right is passed as the path runs on by the summit cairn. *From the cairn its illustrious neighbours the Langdale Pikes are little more than a stone's throw away, yet appear curiously insignificant from behind the scenes.*

Though the main path continues straight on, for Harrison Stickle leave Thunacar Knott's cairn by a choice of thinner paths bound for the saddle in front of the rock tor before that peak. Near a couple of pools a clearer path goes left for the short rise onto Pavey Ark, a dependable series of cairns guiding the path across a veritable boulderfield, then passing through an old wall just before gaining the summit cairn. *With half of Stickle Tarn visible below, this is a dramatic moment.*

Leave on the same path, returning to the pools and picking up the path coming down off Thunacar Knott. This now skirts the right side of the tor to reach a high saddle under the rocky summit of Harrison Stickle. A five-minute clamber will have the summit underfoot, and it lives up to the fell's general appeal. To south and east crags guard the top, and it is from here that the most dramatic views are obtained. *Three very different features earn a mention, first being an aerial view of Langdale's green floor curving away towards the silvery waters of Windermere; next is a side-on picture of Pavey Ark hovering above Stickle Tarn; and third an outstanding array of lofty peaks hemming in this special dalehead.*

Retrace steps to the minor saddle between the summit and the small rock tor. At a path junction here turn left for Pike o'Stickle, descending easy ground to meet another path just short of the stream in the amphitheatre of Harrison Combe. Cross straight over the stream and remain on the path bound directly for Pike o'Stickle. It rises to the head of a great stone shoot that was once a classic Lakeland scree-run: now run out, it is not recommended as a descent route.

Pike o'Stickle's graceful cone thrusts itself skyward from the mass of the mountainside and the cliffs wrapped around it, and the final climb is an exhilarating little scramble. The normal route climbs right before clambering back up the rocky top, though an earlier branch left is a shade easier and more direct. The neat top greets you with a sense of airiness rarely found on Lakeland summits. *This is a place to soak up atmosphere while lapping up two outstanding examples of mountain architecture supplied by Gimmer Crag on neighbouring Loft Crag, and Bowfell asserting its full height from Mickleden to summit cairn.*

Return to the base of the summit lump and go east on the path skirting the head of the scree run, rising over gentle knolls onto Loft Crag. *This is the third of the Langdale Pikes, a less famous cousin of the exalted Stickle brothers, which are displayed better from here than from any other single vantage point. It also boasts one of Langdale's best known cliffs and a charming summit. The rockface in question is Gimmer Crag, a climbers' favourite that falls away only a short distance below the summit area, which is a tiny perch high above a seemingly vertical plunge into Mickleden.*

Continue east along the short crest, the path at the end dropping left onto easier ground, but from the very end a downward scramble is needed to reach the grassy knoll below. A couple of minutes further and a large cairn in the lowest point marks a path junction. Just in front is the cairned top of Thorn Crag, while the Harrison Stickle path comes in from the left. Here turn sharp right on what immediately becomes a stony, eroded path. This is one of the major Langdales paths, which happily improves in character before too long.

Descending with care, the way slants left beneath a ruin and onto a sloping grassy plateau. Harrison Stickle's summit re-appears to the left. Just short of an abrupt knoll the path swings right to recommence the descent in earnest. It drops to an airy stance above the gullies of Middlefell Buttress, then enjoys a brief terrace along to the left. Running across to a position looking to the great gash of Dungeon Ghyll, just in front, the path then spirals down - featuring one particularly rough section - to improve as it nears the foot of the ravine: there is a super prospect of the main waterfall. Cross the stream to join another path, and from the stile turn down the wallside path to a kissing-gate. Go left to descend the final enclosure to return to the start.

Middlefell Farm, Dungeon Ghyll, looking to Bowfell

DUNGEON GHYLL TO KESWICK

DISTANCE *15 miles (24km)*

ORDNANCE SURVEY MAPS
1:50,000
Landranger 89 - West Cumbria
or
Landranger 90 - Penrith, Keswick & Ambleside
1:25,000
Explorer OL6 - English Lakes South West
Explorer OL4 - English Lakes North West

This stage is the very heart of Lakeland, leaving Langdale by way of a splendid mountain pass, followed by a magical walk along the green floor of Borrowdale and by Derwentwater

Return to the rear of the Old Hotel, and rise left to the gate from where you came down. *Above you is the big wall of Raven Crag, a climbers' favourite, while below is Middlefell Farm.* A splendid track heads along the valley floor, soon between widely-spaced walls. *Savour to the full these glorious surrounds dominated by mighty Bowfell.* Emerging onto the foot of the fell at successive kissing-gates by sheep-folds, the left-hand wall remains company a little further until leaving you alone in this wonderful basin of Mickleden, very much a cul-de-sac for non-hillwalkers! Simply advance along the dale floor amid the grandeur of the mountains. *To the right is a worn-out scree run under Pike o'Stickle's summit cone, only a few decades ago discovered to be the location of a Neolithic axe factory: the product was so good it was exported great distances.*

The path ultimately runs, latterly in the company of Mickleden Beck, to a simple footbridge over Stake Gill alongside a stone sheep-fold. Here a painted rock advises of the junction you have reached. While the route ahead runs on a little further before facing up to the rigours of Rossett Gill, your way turns immediately right up the far bank of Stake Gill. The path quickly becomes clear again in the bracken, at once beginning the first of countless zigzags of the Stake Pass.

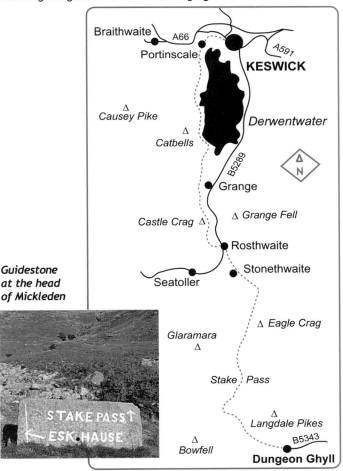

Braithwaite

A66

Portinscale

A591

KESWICK

△
Causey Pike

△
Catbells

Derwentwater

B5289

△
N

Grange

△ *Grange Fell*

Castle Crag △

Rosthwaite

**Guidestone
at the head
of Mickleden**

Stonethwaite

Seatoller

△ *Eagle Crag*

Glaramara
△

Stake Pass

△
Langdale Pikes

B5343

△
Bowfell

Dungeon Ghyll

STAKE PASS ↑
← ESK HAUSE

The Stake Pass is first of three notable ascents on the Cumbria Way, the others being out of Keswick and onto High Pike in Stage 4. This time-honoured way linking Lakeland's best valleys of Langdale and Borrowdale was once a busy packhorse route. By following the zigzags you will save both yourself and the landscape a good deal of stress, for this clever path, with its various paved sections, is as effortless as you could wish for. At the top of the steeper section, the gentle upper stage to the watershed is revealed across the bowl of Langdale Combe. This upland basin is awash with a remarkable array of moraines, left by retreating glaciers at the end of the last Ice Age. The path crosses the stream and resumes along the right side of these hummocks: over and around them it quickly deals with the last bit of climbing to arrive at a cross-paths on the very watershed, marked by a 'summit' cairn just a few steps beyond.

At 1575ft/480m this is by far the highest point yet reached, and appropriately is the major turning point in that all streams hitherto have flown south to Morecambe Bay (by way of Crake or Leven), while from here on they aim northwards to find their way into the Solway Firth (by Derwent or Caldew). The extensive mountain panorama includes the soon to disappear Langdale pairing of Crinkle Crags and mighty Bowfell, along with Esk Pike, Allen Crags, Glaramara, Skiddaw, Lonscale Fell and part of Blencathra: only the cone of Pike o'Stickle represents our erstwhile favourites, the Langdale Pikes.

The start of the descent into Langstrath is initially gentle. *It is comparatively little used as not many folk attempt the Langdale Pikes 'from behind', given the return mileage from Borrowdale in contrast to the vertical directness of Langdale!* A defined edge is soon reached looking down the adjacent Stake Beck and ahead into Langstrath. Here steeper ground is met, though the path again engages useful zigzags to ease the way down alongside some nice waterfalls. Lower down a long waterslide provides company as the path eases and returns to grassiness for the final stage to the valley floor. It runs on to a footbridge on Stake Beck, with Langstrath Beck just a little further downstream. Ignoring a bridge down on the main beck, the path heads off past a lone tree, commencing a lengthy walk along the floor of Langstrath. *The 'Lang Strath' is Scottish in character as well as name: this is indeed a very long valley by Lakeland standards, having already run more than two miles from the stream's beginnings as Allencrags Gill under the shadow of Esk Pike.*

Shortly after the beck makes a big swing from beneath distinctive Cam Crag ridge across the dale, a stile is reached in the first wall met. Immediately after crossing, go left the few yards to appraise Blackmoss Pot, where the beck tumbles down a fall to be forced into a short but delectable ravine, with vertical rock walls and a very deep, very clear pool. Don't fall in though. The path resumes with an adjacent fence or wall for company, and the beck some distance away. This remains so for some time, beneath the rough flanks of Sergeant's Crag and along to a bridle-gate in a wall corner under Eagle Crag.

Just a little further is another opportunity to trade banks. This footbridge sees paths on either bank re-unite, with the opposite one giving a more direct route to Stonethwaite. The main way continues across marshy ground, on through a bridle-gate to a stone-built path close by the lively beck, and just ahead towards its confluence with Greenup Gill. A footbridge leads over the gill to witness the formation of Stonethwaite Beck. Across it is a bridle-gate where you merge with the Greenup path, and turn downstream past sheepfolds. *Here you also meet the celebrated Coast to Coast Walk, a joint campaign that lasts only as far as Rosthwaite.*

Descending the Stake Pass into Langstrath

Beyond a couple of inflowing streams and a bridle-gate, calmer going ensues. Partly enclosed by walls the path runs on, a glimpse of Stonethwaite ahead being first sign of habitation since Dungeon Ghyll. Beyond another bridle-gate this lovely way marches on, at times open by the beck, then beneath richly wooded flanks, then enclosed again before passing beneath a sheepfold on a knoll to arrive at a fork where you can opt to visit Stonethwaite. *To do so, simply go left along the walled way to bridge the beck, and into a most picturesque vision of civilisation. Stonethwaite is an idyllic, archetypal Lakeland hamlet with the Langstrath Country Inn, refreshments and a popular campsite.*

The main way continues on the east bank alongside a wall, soon passing through a gate to become enclosed, often in the company of Stonethwaite Beck to lead delightfully on to a lane on the edge of Rosthwaite. Turn left over the bridge and along to the B5289 valley road, going left into the village. *Tiny Rosthwaite is Borrowdale's focal point, for it features its only true shop and pub, the Scafell Hotel, along with a youth hostel at nearby Longthwaite. For several centuries Borrowdale was mined for plumbago, discovered just a couple of miles up the main valley at Seathwaite, which gave rise to Keswick's once famous pencil industry. Mining peaked two centuries ago, ultimately losing out, as with so many such products, to cheap foreign imports.*

Leave the village by the narrow lane opposite the shop, past the car park to Yew Tree Farm tearoom. Through the yard a rough lane runs to the River Derwent. *This is the Cumbria Way's first encounter with this beautiful mountain river formed by the meeting of Styhead Gill and Grains Gill in the hills beyond Seathwaite. Its existence is a short but priceless one, continuing beyond Derwentwater to soon lose its identity in Bassenthwaite Lake.*

At the river remain on the track downstream to the stone arched New Bridge, with a backdrop formed by the irrepressible Castle Crag. *This volcanic upthrust created one of the district's real gems, and is a prime example of the old adage that size isn't everything. Its modest stature is a positive advantage given its location, for in Lakeland's most beautiful valley it is a perfect eminence from which to survey the charms of the dale and still gain a perspective of the surrounding mountains: the fellwalk from Grange visits its top.*

Cross the bridge and resume down the other bank to quickly reach a pair of gates. Take the right one and follow the track. While most people simply remain on this as it swings left through an open pasture and along to enter a wood, the true footpath keeps faith with the river, within yards reaching the confluence of our old friend Stonethwaite Beck with the Derwent, a super spot where the identical becks merge to form a deep, clear pool. Simply trace the newly strengthened river along the pasture to find a stile into the wood at the end, and a thin path runs to join the broad main path.

The broad path runs on through dense woodland, soon drifting away from the Derwent. At an early fork an unofficial branch goes right to the river, but the main path loses it for some time, engulfed in delightful woodland. Just past the dark chasm of an old slate quarry, you pass through a gateway and spoil heaps at a clearing to rise the short way through trees to a junction. The lesser left branch goes off to inspect more quarried caves, while the main path runs grandly on and gently down, and passing through another gateway it drops down to a clearing on the valley floor. All that's missing is the Derwent, and the crystal-clear river duly glides in amid tranquil but grand scenery between Castle Crag and Grange Fell, the 'Jaws of Borrowdale'.

A little further, through a gate the path drops down to join a broader bridle-track at a wide bend in the river. Bear right on this, over two footbridges and rapidly losing the Derwent's company to emerge from the woods at a gate. Remain on this wide wallside track past Hollows Farm campsite to a junction. While the Cumbria Way omits Grange, few walkers will wish to do so. *For Grange, turn right for a short, easy stroll into the village centre, where you will find riverside tea gardens, the Holy Trinity church, and a long, low double-arched bridge spanning the wide-flowing Derwent. Grange in Borrowdale is the little-used Sunday name. On leaving, don't cross the bridge but go left on the road out, soon passing the Borrowdale Gates Hotel.*

The Cumbria Way turns left at the Hollows fork for a short stroll to the farm. *This was a homely outpost of the youth hostel 'family' for no less than forty years. The author sampled it on a first hostelling trip in 1973, its last year of operation: sadly a farmhouse without self-catering facilities fits less easily into the modern YHA set-up.* Bear right past the buildings and out on an enclosed track heading away over a tiny stream to a gate. Continue on a grassy track along the base of the open fell to the very corner in front of a wood. From the right-hand gate follow the delightful thin path over a scrubby pasture to a small gate onto the road near the Borrowdale Gates Hotel. You have now by-passed Grange, which is just minutes back along to the right.

At the Borrowdale Gates the direct route through Grange rejoins the official route. Remain on the road for a quarter-hour until some farm buildings on the right, and just a little further take a gate on the right signed to Lodore. A firm track heads away in the company of Ellers Beck, on the right. *Catbells rises provocatively over to the left.* When the stream parts company the track crosses the field centre to the far corner, where a kissing-gate sends a fieldside path off alongside bracken to a kissing-gate into more open country near the head of Derwentwater. At an immediate fork go left, onto a minor brow to reveal the lake just ahead. At the next fork bear right to quickly drop down onto a main path alongside the lakeshore at Great Bay. *This southernmost point of the lake is a lovely spot to linger, with the lofty northern mountains of Skiddaw and Blencathra seen beyond its farthest shore.*

The heart of Borrowdale, looking to the Stonethwaite Valley

Turn left on the path which remains within view of the lake as it runs through scattered birch woodland and bracken, at times on boards to protect the fragile habitat. Ignoring lesser paths keep on to enter the woodland of Manesty Park through a gate in a wall. The path runs over labyrinthine tree roots to the idyllic inlet of Myrtle Bay, then continues over a tiny bridge to run a more defined course to the larger Abbot's Bay. On through fine oaks the path quickly joins a firm access road opposite the cottage of The Warren. Turn right along this which ends at a gate ahead. Bear right past the lone white house of Brandelhow, and just over a stream turn right to a small gate back on Derwentwater's shore at Brandelhow Bay. *Skiddaw and Blencathra rise impressively ahead, and tomorrow you'll pass between them.*

A path swings round the edge of spoil heaps from an old lead mine and on into trees behind, passing High Brandelhow landing stage. *This is the first of four stages the Way passes in the next 2½ miles. If desired you could opt to reach Keswick in style on one of the popular launches, much as at Coniston: a regular seasonal service sees them plying the lake in both directions (there are seven landing stages in total), so you can't fail to reach Keswick!*

Simply remain on this delectable lakeshore route through the trees, passing a novel woodland carving from 2002, commemorating 100 years of the National Trust at Brandelhow. At the next landing stage, Low Brandelhow, pass through a gate out of the trees and the firm path forks. The Way remains on the main path which bears left to a small gate between a belt of trees, where the rambling lakeshore path comes back in after embracing the small headland. Through the gate the path runs round to the right to rejoin the lakeshore, briefly, as far as a superb seat carved from a dead tree. From here the track swings left up the pasture to a gate onto an access road. Follow this right, past an outdoor activity centre and along to a junction at Hawse End. *Along the short lane to the right is Hawse End landing stage.*

Take a kissing-gate on the right immediately after the junction, and a well-worn path heads off through woodland. It drops down to a footbridge into an open pasture, The Park, which offers a splendid look back to Catbells and the knobbly crest of Causey Pike. At the other end a gate sees the path back into trees, eventually emerging onto the drive to Lingholm. *Lingholm boasts an enviable position, its grounds reaching down to the shore of Derwentwater and attracting visitors to walk amongst the shrubbery and laid-out woodlands.*

Cross straight over the drive to a broad path heading away with a wall into the woods. As the wall quickly swings away to the right, a more direct path through the trees of Fawe Park forges straight on to meet the road to Portinscale, but the better option is to stay with the path by the wall. At the other end of Fawe Park's greenery a drive is met: crossing straight over the path drops left into the bustle of Nichol End, with boatyard, landing stage, shop and cafe on Derwentwater's shore. Go left along the short lane to meet the Portinscale road only yards beyond the emergence of the direct path. Turn right for the short walk into Portinscale, with a footway most of the way. *By-passed by the A66, Portinscale stands at the entrance to the Newlands Valley and near the foot of Derwentwater, sufficiently distant from Keswick to maintain an air of tranquillity. Its pub, the Farmers, is along to the left on the edge of the village. It also has a tearoom/giftshop.*

At the main junction in the village bear right as the main road swings left, on past the imposing Derwentwater Hotel before coming to the road's abrupt demise. Advance to cross a sizeable suspension foot-bridge on the Derwent, which has just been fortified by the additional waters of Keswick's river, the Greta. Across the bridge, advance a short way along the road, but shortly take a gate on the right which sends a direct, enclosed hard path along a couple of fields into Keswick town, sat directly ahead, backed by Clough Head and the Dodds ridge. The path emerges alongside a bridge on the Greta, opposite the old pencil works. Turn right for a short stroll into the centre.

Keswick-on-Derwentwater is the capital of Northern Lakeland. From here roads radiate to many of the principal lakes, but the one that Keswick boasts as the best is its own Derwentwater, which laps up to the edge of town. Dubbed 'Queen of the English Lakes', it forms a formidable threesome with Keswick and Skiddaw, the northernmost 3000-foot mountain which rises grandly behind town and lake. Just a little downstream of Derwentwater, Bassenthwaite Lake is the third largest and most northerly of the English Lakes. Just above it on the wooded flanks of Skiddaw, Cumbria's first ospreys in over 150 years have returned to breed. Our only fish-eating bird of prey is obviously very happy with the contents of Bassenthwaite!

Keswick stands on the banks of the River Greta, and its central feature is a sloping main street across which a host of shops and pubs face each other. More recently the number of pubs has dwindled while the number of outdoor shops has increased. In the market place is the historic, island-like Moot Hall, partly used as an information centre. Probably Keswick's most important building is Greta Hall, for 40 years the home of Poet Laureate Robert Southey, where he played host to a procession of contemporaries, including Wordsworth himself.

Perhaps surprisingly Keswick played a major part in the pencil industry, for graphite from Borrowdale's plumbago mines gave the town the world's first pencil factory. Still producing the goods - though in the care of a larger firm and without local ingredients - the Cumberland Pencil Company and its 'Lakeland' pencils will be long remembered. An interesting pencil museum is on the premises, while there are also the Keswick Museum with its great model of Lakeland that took 17 years to create, and the Keswick Mining Museum too. For its size Keswick has the greatest number of B&Bs in the country, so accommodation should not be a problem - it also has a youth hostel overlooking Fitz Park. At one time the mid-point on a railway linking the market towns of Cockermouth and Penrith, Keswick lost its last rail link in 1972, the Cockermouth section having disappeared in 1966. Roads took over here with a vengeance when the A66, joining those same towns, by-passed Keswick: now lorries bound for the west coast rumble under the foot of Skiddaw and on concrete bridges over the Greta Gorge, when with little extra effort they could have by-passed the entire National Park further north.

Derwentwater at Nichol End, looking to Latrigg

A FELLWALK FROM GRANGE

DISTANCE *7 miles/11km*   ASCENT *2575ft/785m*

SUMMITS
Castle Crag	*951ft/290m*	High Spy	*2142ft/653m*
Maiden Moor	*1889ft/576m*	Catbells	*1479ft/451m*

ORDNANCE SURVEY MAPS
1:50,000 - Landranger 89 or Landranger 90
1:25,000 - Explorer OL4

Grange is served from Keswick by the Borrowdale bus. Leave Grange on a lane heading south out of the village centre, alongside a cafe and just before the church. This is the drive to Hollows Farm and bridleway towards Seatoller. It leads to a junction by open ground just before which Castle Crag is revealed ahead as a wooded knoll. Here the farm road swings right, and a wide track advances straight on through a gate and into woods to join the Derwent. After successive footbridges on inflowing streams, a guidepost signals the point to leave the river and take the right fork. This climbs steadily through trees, alongside a small stream which is soon crossed before breaking out into more open country between woodland and bracken-covered fellside.

As height is gained the lofty Goat Crag on High Spy and Castle Crag's own impressive cliffs form mighty portals above your deep trench. An old sheepfold with a massive corner boulder is passed, while the view back reveals Derwentwater and Skiddaw. The stream is re-crossed, and as the scree on the left recedes the brow of the old road is neared. Before re-crossing to the right bank of the stream a massive cairn in this grassy amphitheatre signifies the point of departure for a short and memorable detour onto Castle Crag.

This begins by curving up to the top of a small tor on the left. Here will be found a stile in a wall, and a clear path climbs steeply past a memorial seat up to another wall-stile at the foot of scree slopes. At these slate quarry remains the main path bears right, spiralling up to a cairn at the bottom of a vast spoil heap. A firmly trodden path zigzags up the mountain of slate in surprisingly easy fashion, to arrive at a platform with slate cairns overlooking an exquisite panorama of upper Borrowdale. Behind them is the surprisingly extensive quarry site, with the path climbing to its right to gain the grassy summit plateau.

A major highlight is the sudden view north, as the Derwent glides past the white-walled houses of Grange, leading to Derwentwater backed by Skiddaw. The highest point is a great cairn atop a large mound of rock to which is affixed a memorial tablet, with the lip of the quarry encroaching dangerously close. While savouring this classic summit, it can easily be envisaged as the ancient British hillfort it once was. A more fitting location could not exist for a memorial to the Borrowdale men lost in the Great War. Retrace steps to the main route.

Resuming on the main route, the track continues steadily up to gain the col severing Castle Crag from High Spy. *Here Derwentwater is traded for the head of Borrowdale, with Glaramara dominant along with the giants of Great End and Broad Crag with the summit of Scafell Pike sneaking in.* Ignoring a grassy path slanting down to a gate, the track contours delightfully around the fellside to a major fork. While the left branch is the bridleway, the broad continuing track is your way.

Keep right on this higher way (an old mine road), still largely level as it approaches the side gill of Tongue Gill. *Rosthwaite sits on the green floor of Borrowdale beneath Great Crag, with part of the Helvellyn range already appearing behind.* The track starts to rise into the gill, soon climbing to a gate in a fence. Ahead on the other flank are the extensive remains of Rigghead Quarries. Through the gate you can opt to remain on this bank, though the usual route crosses the stream to a similar path on the other bank. This rises to the foot of the mining area, where the north bank path, which displays some fine embanked sections of the old quarry way, now crosses the beck too. Pass through a stile here and resume up the south bank.

Soon the path starts to rise away from the beck through the lower limits of the upper quarry site. This grand path climbs past ruins and several levels and forbidding entrances amid vast spoil heaps. The quarry site ends abruptly and a contrastingly normal path heads away, rising gently towards a fence just above. Approaching it the way forks at a cairn, with Dale Head's upper slopes set back behind. Ignore the stile above and take the path traversing right to a stile in a right-angle of the fence. Across a tiny stream the faint path rises gently left to commence a steady rise all the way onto High Spy's top.

Open views now look back south to the Scafells and Great Gable, with a glimpse of nearby Dalehead Tarn. At one point the path swings left beneath a small rash of stones: the branch ahead quickly leads to the main path near the Newlands edge, but better to take the right branch resuming the ascent to arrive at a skyline cairn. This reveals the true summit cairn just minutes away, a steady rise to the fine top. *This splendid cairn sits just a short way from the steep westerly plunge into the lovely Newlands Valley, which is backed by the sudden revelation of the delectable ridges and tops of the north-western fells based on Grasmoor.*

Resume north on the broad path high above Newlands. As this undulates along, Derwentwater makes its first proper appearance. An early fork at a slight rise sees the right branch cross to the cairned top of Blea Crag (a superb viewpoint for the environs of Grange) before returning to the main western branch. This now drops onto the slender Narrow Moor, a grand moment as Grange appears. The path skirts above steep heathery plunges then forks as it moves onto Maiden Moor. The right branch is most direct, but the left branch is more rewarding as it climbs negligibly to the Newlands edge to run along to the tiniest of scrappy cairns marking the marginal summit of Maiden Moor. *This is a good place to take stock of the glorious prospect immediately to your west, dominated by the northern ridges of neighbouring Hindscarth and Robinson. Ahead rises the knobbly prow of little Catbells, backed by the lakes of Derwentwater and Bassenthwaite and the northern giants of Skiddaw and Blencathra.*

Resume again, a thin path soon branching right to rejoin the near-by main path. This slants down to the Borrowdale edge, being wide, stony and a little steeper as it prepares to drop onto Hause Gate. Derwentwater is now fully revealed in expansive loveliness. The dip of Hause Gate marks a crossroads of ridge-path with inter-valley path. Ahead sits Catbells, which on a nice day really demands you undertake the short pull onto a classic Lakeland mini-fell, even though the onward route is back to Hause Gate. The well used path makes light work of the climb to Catbells' cairn, which you will be lucky to have to yourself.

Descend from Hause Gate by turning left (or right if you omitted Catbells!), the restored path at once becoming steep. Initially zigzags wind down the upper section, to be replaced by a long, unbroken slant. Ignore a branch left part way down, and simply remain on this slant with a glimpse of Grange part way down, continuing on to merge with a terrace path coming in from the left. The path continues down the lower section to a gate in a fence. Don't cross the fence but turn right on a permissive path above it, merging with a public path at the end. This rises outside a house at Manesty, quickly turning left to run a level course through pines above a deer fence. From a stile at the end, open country at the foot of Maiden Moor is entered. *Grange Fell, Castle Crag and Glaramara are well seen behind.*

Beyond a cluster of tiny footbridges in a moist corner, the path runs a splendid course above the intake wall. Further on are a couple of forks. You can use either as the branches re-unite before reaching a footbridge on the appreciable stream of Ellers Beck. This brings you back to the intake wall. Just beyond is a stile alongside a covered tank, from where bear left down the rough pasture, with Grange just ahead now. Take the gate in the very corner and follow the thin path across a pasture to a small gate onto the road near the Borrowdale Gates Hotel. Turn right for a couple of minutes back into the village.

Castle Crag from the Cumbria Way alongside the River Derwent

KESWICK TO CALDBECK

DISTANCE 15 miles (24km)
(including alternative western route: 17 or 17^{1}2 miles/27km or 28km)

ORDNANCE SURVEY MAPS
1:50,000
Landranger 90 - Penrith, Keswick & Ambleside
1:25,000
Explorer OL4 - English Lakes North West
Explorer OL5 - English Lakes North East

> *This last Lakeland stage has most climbing, though it is split into two different halves, and the walking through the rounded hills 'back o'Skidda' is largely very easy and relaxing*

NOTE BEFORE STARTING: In case of bad weather or a general desire to escape the hills, an alternative route breaks off at Skiddaw House, following the old supply road out of the hills to plot a gentler course around the base of the northern fells, largely on quiet roads and farm tracks. The mileage is greater (by between 2 and 2^{1}2 miles), and the surroundings are less impressive: nevertheless it can serve a useful purpose.

Leave the Moot Hall in the Market Place by way of St John's Street at the top corner, then keep left on Station Street and straight over the main road onto Station Road. This crosses the Greta and runs past Fitz Park: at the far end keep straight on up the short rise to the entrance to Keswick Spa, at the site of the old railway station. Just behind, its car park gives access to Brundholme Road. Turn left (taking advantage of a footway) as far as the modern houses at Briar Rigg, with Latrigg directly above and the Skiddaw massif to its left. Here strike off right on Spooney Green Lane, climbing to bridge the incongruous by-pass. Sanity is restored as it climbs past the lone house at Spooney Green and through a gate into the bottom corner of Latrigg Woods. The path climbs steeply up the wood edge, but mercifully the gradient soon relents. Ignore any paths that strike out to the right bound for Latrigg's summit: all should be refused in favour of the main highway with its views across to Skiddaw beyond open gorse banks. *Sections of both Bassenthwaite Lake and Derwentwater can be seen, while the north-western fells are dominated by the graceful cone of Grisedale Pike.*

After woodland on the left ends, the path swings out into more open country, and you climb to join a wider track on the forest edge. Just a little higher the way curves up as two separate lanes, briefly: as

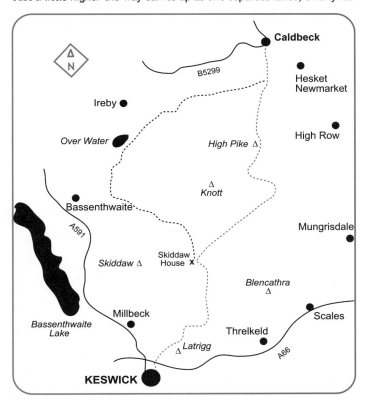

the left one swings right back across ours, simply advance straight up. The super path continues rising to approach another forest corner. Just a little further, ignore a fork left into Gale Ghyll Woods. *This dark, extensive plantation from the early 1960s denies any views, though parts are now being felled.* Ultimately the path emerges at a gate onto the terminus of the surfaced Gale Road. *This is a popular start point for the ascent of Skiddaw, or a contrastingly brief stroll onto Latrigg.*

Turn right through the car park, and at the end pass through a gate. Turn immediately left on the wallside path, on through a kissing-gate and on the fenceside to a kissing-gate onto the open fell. *Visible off-route just ahead is the Hawell monument, a cross commemorating members of a local shepherding family.* The Cumbria Way, however, breaks off the Skiddaw 'tourist' path by bearing right from the gate. This quickly drops to ford Whit Beck, before an equally steady slant back out. *From here on you will enjoy first-class, near-level walking for a good couple of hours as far as the road-end in Mosedale.*

The north-western fells from the Cumbria Way under Lonscale Fell

The path now runs a grand course on the lower flank of Lonscale Fell, with super views south to the Helvellyn range, as well as back to the Borrowdale and north-western fells. Eventually the path swings left to a gate in a fence. This transfer from the open Lakes to the recesses of Skiddaw Forest is a grand moment, and quite exciting. *Ahead is the heathery cone of Great Calva, the sentinel of Skiddaw Forest. The title Skiddaw Forest is an ancient name: it is a considerable time since trees flourished here, other than the cluster sheltering Skiddaw House.*

The path runs north along the much more robust eastern slope of Lonscale Fell, with the deep gouge of the Glenderaterra Valley below. *This present section beneath the modest fractures of Lonscale Crags is one of the very finest on the entire Way.* Curving up to a small footbridge the path runs by remains of buildings from quarrying times. Exactly as a broader way comes up from the right close by a wall, a 'Guide Stone' indicated on the map is passed. *This is simply a large pathside boulder on which 'Keswick' and an arrow have been inscribed, with fading paint.* Resume on the broader path continuing above the wall, which soon fades as the path runs on beneath Lonscale Fell's Burnt Horse ridge to reach the Glenderaterra-Caldew watershed, ending at a gate in a fence at some 1378ft/420m.

Immediately through this you enter a heather zone, the basin of Skiddaw Forest is scooped at your feet, and more usefully the lonely outpost of Skiddaw House makes its appearance beneath its shelter belt of trees and surrounding old enclosures, with mighty Skiddaw's summit ridge high to its left. The path drops to a wooden footbridge on Salehow Beck then gently rises to Skiddaw House. *On a knoll at some 1542ft/470m, Skiddaw House is Lakeland's highest habitable stone building. Built as a shooting lodge it became a shepherd's bothy until the late 1960s: after a spell as a schools' outdoor centre in the 1970s it stood empty for some years before finding a seemingly perfect role as a simple youth hostel in 1987. Only the efforts of a handful of enthusiasts kept the place running, and by 2003 it again stood empty. Somehow, this is unlikely to be the end of the Skiddaw House story...*

Now is decision time as the western alternative departs from here. The only really relevant factor will normally be the conditions. If you don't want to ascend to over 2000ft on High Pike, take the alternative. But bear in mind that you're already at three-quarters of that altitude here, so it's hardly going to be a major mountaineering ascent. Consider too that the alternative is longer and generally harder on the feet. As you won't save yourself any time or effort, then it would seem that only abysmal weather should deter you from High Pike, the best and direct route. For the alternative turn to page 61, otherwise carry on below.

At the gateway in the wall beneath the house, the alternative path bears left to merge into the service track. The main route, however, turns sharp right through the gateway onto a broad path descending through heather alongside the wall. *Carrock Fell makes a distinctive objective some miles in that direction, and will remain so until at its foot.* The wall turns off but the path continues down to a footbridge on the youthful Caldew. The path rises briefly before commencing a long, near-level march along the base of Great Calva. Though any route description is unnecessary, several interesting features merit comment.

A sturdy, circular stone sheepfold is passed, then further along, the major side valley of Wiley Gill is marked by the sudden appearance of an identical sheepfold alongside. A footbridge crosses the beck and a stile crosses the fence descending from Great Calva, to resume as before. Now on the base of massive Knott, heather and bracken lead on past a ruined fold, then a square one with an old stone hut, then a solitary tree makes a rare landmark. The lively river briefly closes in, and after the deep-cut Burdell Gill ignore a left fork, as a Landrover track now runs on through a narrower section, across the smaller Wet Swine Gill and unfailingly along to a stone arched bridge on Grainsgill Beck, and the terminus of a surfaced road in the valley of Mosedale.

Your spell on tarmac lasts only a few steps. Across the bridge, head straight up a path in front to join the old road built to serve the Carrock Mine. Turn left up this into the colourful valley of Grainsgill. At once the old mine is seen ahead, while above the dalehead your objective of the lonely Lingy Hut is silhouetted on the skyline. For now, the mine road leads gently and quickly to the mining site at the confluence with Brandy Gill. It is important to remember that hidden dangers lurk for those who stray from the paths. *The Carrock Mine was a very rare source of wolfram, from which tungsten was produced. Begun as a mid-19th century search for lead, its prolific period was during World War One, when up to 100 men worked the site; it had a brief revival during World War Two, as tungsten was used in armaments.*

Almost opposite the main buildings ignore a fork left to cross the beck to them, but use the old green way continuing to slant gently up. As this curves to the right, consider a choice of routes to the Lingy Hut, the official route by the beck, or the direct route running further north.

• For the mapped route, take the continuing way which now slants down to Grainsgill Beck. Don't cross, but turn upstream on a thin but generally clear and pleasant path. At times a little rough, its largely undemanding course soon reaches the confluence with Arm o'Grain flowing in from the right. This is a charming little spot overlooked by a solitary tree. Across Arm o'Grain resume as before, past a waterfall and easing out to arrive at Miller Moss on the edge of the high plateau. In this marshy corner a better cross-path is met. Turn right on this for an improving stroll and short rise to Lingy Hut.

• The easier bee-line to the hut is as follows. Instead of dropping to the bank of the gill, rise gently right onto the start of a wide shelf well above the beck. A distinct broad path is quickly joined, running a largely level course through bracken to arrive at the sidestream of Arm o'Grain. Cross to some low ruins, and the narrower but clear path climbs steadily through bracken, never far from the stream on your right. After steepening, the stream swings further right and the path forges more directly up the grassy fell, steeper again but very good as it relents to reach a distinctive isolated boulder. Precisely here, the Lingy Hut returns to view, happily just a short, gentle stroll further.

High Pike, summit of the Cumbria Way, looking to Blencathra

The former shooters' cabin of Lingy Hut is a useful shelter from the elements, and is maintained as a bothy by the National Park Authority. A visitors book gives evidence of its popularity. Resume north on the old shooters' track, passing beneath fenced sheepfolds and then rising over the rounded top of Hare Stones. From here High Pike finally reveals itself in front as a rounded grassy dome. The track drops very gently down, and as its intention of slanting to the right of your objective becomes clear, take an initially faint path breaking off left in this modest saddle for a steady, effortless pull onto the felltop. It fades just before reaching it, though if desired you could bear right to join a broader path ascending from a little further along the old track.

With High Pike's summit underfoot, you may be astonished by the presence of a slate memorial seat, behind which is located an Ordnance Survey column and an immense, sprawling cairn and shelter. At 2158ft/658m High Pike is Lakeland's northernmost 2000-footer, and given that you've just walked the length of Lakeland, it is odd indeed that only at the very end should you breast a mountain summit! A study of the view might largely be directed at the miles of farmland stretching into the haze of infinity, though the Scafell group slots neatly in between the bulky fells across Skiddaw Forest.

Resume north to find, within a hundred yards, the depleted ruin of a shepherd's hut, offering further shelter and a view of Caldbeck. *It is to Caldbeck that High Pike gives allegiance.* The 'official' route towards waiting Caldbeck suggests you simply make a bee-line slightly east of north, though I recommend a much better clear path to follow. Ignore a distinct quad track bearing right down the fell towards the two wind turbines visible beyond, and instead bear correspondingly left of Caldbeck (slightly west of north), virtually at once finding yourself on a splendid path. This descends the grassy fellside to meet a cross-path just yards short of a saddle in front of a rounded knoll. Turn right on this, soon slanting gently down above the very beginnings of Potts Gill.

Potts Gill's mining history becomes immediately evident, another reminder that hidden dangers lurk off the paths. Just past a spoil heap, fork left on another distinct branch which descends parallel with the gill - back on a Caldbeck bee-line through the remains of Potts Gill Mine. Lower down the track swings left beneath a fenced shaft onto a broader old road about to cross the gill. Don't cross but go right a few paces and another main branch drops directly away to resume the descent, now through the main part of the mine site, amid various debris and spoil. *Unlike long abandoned lead mining, the winning of barytes from the old mines continued well into the 20th century. The site was still very active in the 1950s and closed as recently as 1966, so that within living memory an aerial ropeway descended from Potts Gill Mine to loading bays at Nether Row. Remarkably, these Caldbeck Mines feature around 8 miles of levels excavated below your feet.* As the track slants down to the right beneath a spoil heap, a delightful grassy way takes a short-cut down left off it, itself soon bearing right to slant down past a distinctive boulder towards the base of the fell. At a wall corner it rejoins the hard track to run on down to a gate off the hill. Continue along this track into the top end of Nether Row.

Keep left on the track past the first house, its drive continuing out into an area of open ground and junctions in the hamlet. Here the western alternative rejoins the main route. Go straight ahead to the start of the surfaced road, which heads away and slowly drops to a crossroads with The Street. Cross onto a narrow old lane, dropping down and hoping nobody is daft enough to drive up it. Escape at a small patch of open ground, crossing to a stile from where bear left across the field. Pass through a gate and on to a stile right of a house. Joining an enclosed access road, cross to a kissing-gate opposite and head away with the hedge on your left. At the very end drop slightly to a gate in front, and a path winds down a small wooded bank and on to a stone arched footbridge just ahead. Bear right on the hedgerowed path heading away to enter Caldbeck. Turn right for the village centre.

Caldbeck is the National Park's northernmost village, its isolation being a welcome change from the regular tourist honeypots. Its pub is the Oddfellows Arms, which had a time known as the John Peel Inn in deference to Caldbeck's famous son: it was originally the Rising Sun, one of 13 pubs here two centuries ago! Born around 1777, John Peel lived his life close by the village: this farmer who ran his own pack of foxhounds in the first half of the 19th century is remembered as the archetypal Cumbrian huntsman, thanks to being immortalised in song. Though seemingly neither the best huntsman nor the nicest of men, his name lives on thanks to the efforts of John Woodcock Graves, a local man who became a firm friend. Within the surviving pub he penned the celebrated words that would be sung with feeling by Cumbrians the world over. Peel died in 1854 and some 3000 folk attended his funeral: his grave is easily located to the left of the church door.

Also buried at Caldbeck is Mary Robinson, the 'Beauty of Buttermere'. This innkeeper's daughter was bigamously wed by London scoundrel John Hatfield some two centuries ago: he was tried and hanged at Carlisle, and Mary went on to find a happy marriage locally. St Kentigern's church dates back in part to the 13th century, with the tower being from the early 1700s. On the bank behind is St Mungo's Well (Mungo being the Scottish name for Kentigern), stone steps lead down to this supposed holy spring right by the footbridge. Also to be found in Caldbeck are a Post office/shop, tearoom and giftshop, and numerous old houses boasting 17th century dated lintels. Priests Mill, an old watermill on the Cald Beck, dates back 300 years, and restored in 1986 it features a waterwheel along with a restaurant and crafts shops. A former brewery survives at Lord's Mill. Hill farming survives too, of course, whereas the once very important mining industry has entirely disappeared: though its heyday was in the 19th century, the mining of lead and barytes lasted well into the 20th century.

A popular little stroll, easily reached on the edge of the village is to The Howk, where the beck thunders through a limestone gorge. From the car park, pass out of the other end onto a road alongside the green, with its pond. Go left, but at the green corner take a gate into a yard and out the other end on an enclosed path that runs beneath a wooded bank to The Howk bobbin mill. Here stand the restored remains of a coppice shed, where hardwood was stored. A massive waterwheel helped turn seasoned coppice wood into bobbins, and was only dismantled as part of the 1939-45 war effort. Beyond it a path takes over, rising up stone steps to give a smashing view of Whelpo Beck thundering through the limestone walls of the ravine. The path runs above it to a footbridge, across which rise to a kissing-gate into a field, then slant diagonally left across to a corner gate onto the road at Todcroft. Turn left past the school junction and back down into the village. At the next junction go left, down past the old brewery to just short of the bridge: here pass through a yard on the right to a gate. Cross the field downstream to a squeezer-stile into a garden across which you emerge onto the road by the main bridge.

D'ye ken John Peel with his coat so grey?
D'ye ken John Peel at the break of day?
D'ye ken John Peel when he's far, far away
With his hounds and his horn in the morning?

In the heart of the Skiddaw Forest:
Great Calva and a distant Carrock Fell, from Skiddaw House

THE WESTERN ALTERNATIVE ROUTE

From Skiddaw House follow the old service road away, dropping to cross the fledgling Caldew and then commencing a long, straight rise through the heather. It turns left to bridge a stream and rises a little further, then a level section at 1600ft/488m marks the high point as you make this obvious escape from the hills. *This stage is dominated still by the bulk of Skiddaw to your left. Ahead is the little outlying fell of Binsey backed by distant Criffel, an 1868ft/569m landmark across the Solway Firth.* At the end the track winds down to a stone arched bridge on Dash Beck and around to a gate. With the Dash Valley now fully revealed, a rapid descent begins. *Almost at once pause to appraise a super waterfall below the track, this being the uppermost section of Dash Falls, which will not be seen properly for a while.*

The way curves gracefully down beneath the broken cliff of Dead Crags. As the track levels out, look back to find the beautiful Dash Falls (more romantically titled Whitewater Dash) plunging down the hither-to hidden lower section of the ravine. Beyond the end of the crag the track turns through a gate in the intake wall to join the surfaced Dash farm road. Go left along this, through several pastures with

Bassenthwaite Lake appearing ahead. At the end it drops down onto a back road, with the farm at Peter House just to the right.

Though it's easier to simply turn right along the road, bear in mind there's an appreciable tarmac section to come: it would, however, save you a half-mile and a half-hour on the time-consuming section. The true Way crosses the road to a gate, from where bear left off the track heading away. Head down the field centre to a gate in the very bottom, beyond a wooded corner not on the map. Just beyond is a crossroads of bridleways. Turn sharp right alongside the stand of trees, down the fieldside to a gate at the end. With a house over to the left, continue down to a tiny stream at the bottom with a bridle-gate behind. Crossing one last field, Dash Falls and Bassenthwaite Lake are revealed again. Through a bridle-gate at the corner turn down the steep wooded bank, then back through the fence via a gate. A footbridge on Dash Beck leads into a plantation, where turn right up a short-lived track onto a road.

Cross and ascend a steep path through Park Wood above a small stream. Towards the top bear right to a gate out into fields. Turn right on a track fording the stream and along to a gate. Through it turn off left up the field, slightly left of the high point and crossing to a gate and ladder-stile at the end. Now bear right, but instead of dropping by the wall, contour on to the top of the gorse bank, a superb little stretch with the charming Little Tarn below making a super foreground to the Dash Valley, your last view of the falls. At the end drop down the bank and cross to a gate well left of the tarn foot. A wooden farm bridge crosses the tiny outflow, and just a few steps further take a stile in the fence on the left. Ascend the reedy fieldside, ignoring a gate part way and continuing to one at the top. Continue up, ignoring another gate fronting an enclosed track, and along to a gate in the far corner. Just above are the few buildings of Orthwaite. A few steps beyond the stile sits a stumpy waymark: if it still fails to point up the field, bear right towards the central house, locating a hidden wall-stile at the top to put you back onto the road in front of Orthwaite Cottage.

Turn left, passing salmon-coloured Orthwaite Hall whose north-facing frontage must be appraised as you pass. A fine beech hedge sees you out of the hamlet, then the larger tarn of Over Water is revealed below. As the road drops down past it, keep straight on at a crossroads. The quiet road ascends a steep bank looking down on attractive Chapelhouse Reservoir: look back too to Over Water. Rising past the farm at Lowthwaite the road runs down to a dip just before Longlands.

Across the bridge on Longlands Beck take a gate on the right to gain the open fell. Ignore a track dropping right, instead follow the inviting green track ahead, passing beneath Longlands as it rises from the hamlet. Leaving the intake wall this enjoyable ascent continues. At the top the track curves around to its high point, leaving better known Lakeland behind as Over Water and Skiddaw depart the scene. The track runs free of walls to cross Charleton Gill at Charleton Wath (a ford). Across, an intake wall returns and ushers the now firmer track along the base of the fell, soon dropping down to merge with a farm road. Now surfaced, it drops down past Holborn on neat verges to a junction with an unsigned through road at Green Head: turn right.

Crossing an arched bridge marks the end of open fell, and an enclosed section leads away. The attractive hamlet of Branthwaite provides some interest, leaving it by a stone-arched bridge on Roughton Gill. Climbing away from it you pass a former school of 1875 (note the tablet: despite its size, it still provided separate entrances for boys and girls!). At the next hamlet, Fell Side, the Way escapes the road, though remaining on it would get you to Caldbeck more quickly. Immediately after the last building (an outdoor centre) take a walled track doubling back right. This runs to a gate back onto open fell. Take the concrete track rising away and swinging left to a farm, Little Fellside. Don't enter but remain on the base of the fell, where you have two options.

Looking back to the Dash Valley from Little Tarn

• The official way shadows the intake wall, crossing reedy terrain a little above the wall, aiming for the cluster of farm buildings at Potts Gill. The path runs on to find a tiny footbridge and little gate in the corner beyond the buildings. Leaving the fell, drop down the fieldside to a gate on the left after a small outbuilding, crossing a bridge to join the access road at the end of the buildings. Turn right on this and it leads unfailingly out through the fields to enter the hamlet of Nether Row.

• From Little Fellside preferably rise a few steps above the intake wall to locate the start of a good path, initially among reeds. This runs a higher course, slanting down across the fellside to cross Potts Gill shortly before a wall corner well above the eponymous farm. Continue with the wall to a track junction, turning left down the main one and in doing so rejoining the main route of the Way as it leaves the fell to enter Nether Row.

Leave Nether Row by the surfaced road heading away, and you've rejoined the Way for the last mile and a half to Caldbeck - see page 59.

A FELLWALK FROM KESWICK

DISTANCE 10 miles/16km   *ASCENT 3200ft/975m*

SUMMITS
Carl Side   2447ft/746m   *Skiddaw   3054ft/931m*
Little Man 2837ft/865m

ORDNANCE SURVEY MAPS
1:50,000 - Landranger 89 or Landranger 90
1:25,000 - Explorer OL4

From the market place head north on the Cockermouth road, past the pencil museum and the by-pass junction at the Catholic church at High Hill, then as the road swings left forge on the cul-de-sac road to Crosthwaite church, straight ahead. St Kentigern's is Keswick's ancient parish church: the poet Southey is buried here. At the turning circle turn right through a gate to follow a path away between Keswick School's sports fields, becoming enclosed to rise past the end of the school buildings to a kissing-gate on the brow. Revealed at your feet is the by-pass. A thin path slants right down the field to an underpass below the old railway, and head away to a stile accessing the by-pass.

Cross with care and the path heads away opposite, bearing right to a footbridge on a stream and on to a ladder-stile. Bear left across the field to find a stile in a corner part way on, from where a hedgerowed path rises onto the A591 Carlisle road at Thrushwood. Cross to a kissing-gate, then descend a small wooded bank to another gate back into the fields. Head directly away with the fence on your left, and from the gate at the end bear left to a kissing-gate left of the barn in front. The walk's return route from Little Man is clearly seen on the skyline ahead. Resume with a fence on your left, and when it ends turn sharp left with it. Part way along, a small gate takes you into a leafy, enclosed footway. This soon rises between hedges to a gate accessing a ford and slab footbridge. The broader track then leads out onto the road in Applethwaite, a delightful hamlet.

Go right a few steps then left at the junction by the phone box. Passing Applethwaite Farm the road runs to the edge of the hamlet. As it swings right and starts to climb away, turn left into a yard and out by a gate. Head across the field beneath a steeper bank and with wide views south to the north-western fells. Pass through a small gate and on to Low Grove Farm. From a kissing-gate in front the path diverts round to the right, passing behind the house to a kissing-gate back into fields. Resume as before, on to the end where another kissing-gate awaits. Pass left of a modern barn, from where a stile sees a concrete track lead into the farmyard behind. Don't rise to the house, but go straight on through a gate and along a short enclosed way to more farm buildings. Step left into another yard, then on again on the short access track out onto a rising lane. Turn right up to a T-junction in Millbeck.

Turn left, rising gently out of the hamlet but soon double back right on a rough access road. This is also departed just before it enters private grounds at a cattle-grid: from a small gate on the left a steep enclosed path climbs to a kissing-gate onto the base of the open fell. An inviting green way rises away. Remain on the main branch which climbs steeply through bracken to a stile in a fence. Above this the steepness resumes, but with glorious views back over half of Lakeland. The gradients ease as height is gained, and a far nicer ascent leads through swathes of heather and occasional rocks to reach a much appreciated stance on a knoll. Here an old wall is met, and the last chance for any shelter. Resuming, the path climbs through the modest outcrops of White Stones to a landmark boss of rock. Just above this, a lesser path forks left to ascend the true spur, but less demanding is the main path maintaining a steadier pull. The heather only fades near the top, at which point Skiddaw's summit finally appears as you ease onto the summit of Carl Side, marked by a scrappy cairn.

Resume on the path slanting right for a short drop to a col, and a merging of paths by the pool of Carlside Tarn. The final ascent presents itself as a path slants obliquely left across the scree-draped upper flank of Skiddaw. *To your left the shapely Ullock Pike ridge encloses the deep bowl of Southerndale.* Although steeper towards the top, the good path makes relatively light work of things to suddenly ease at a shelter on the airy summit ridge. A two-minute saunter along the broad, high level ridge leads quickly to the popular summit of Skiddaw.

The highest point is crowned by an Ordnance Survey column, with view indicator, cairns and shelters in attendance. The underlying rock is Skiddaw slate, which makes this the district's oldest mountain. Being Lakeland's giant northerly outpost, Skiddaw was in a chain of beacon sites for many centuries. Celebrations after Nelson's victory at Trafalgar were attended by William Wordsworth, among others, and the first publication of this guide coincides with the bicentenary of that momentous event. Skiddaw's isolation from similarly high ground guarantees an excellent picture of Lakeland's various mountain groups to the south. Other aspects of the view vary from the belt of trees sheltering Skiddaw House deep in the bowl of Skiddaw Forest, to an extensive coastline from the Solway Firth out to the Irish Sea, across which the Galloway Hills and the Isle of Man look very close on clear days.

To return, head back south along the high skyline to its well defined southern terminus, with Derwentwater outspread ahead. The path then slants left down the hill to approach a gate in a fence. While the main tourist path passes through to resume its descent, far more rewarding is the inclusion of Little Man at barely no extra effort. So, don't pass through but turn right along the fenceside. Towards the top it turns off, but simply follow the clear path up onto the little top with its scrappy cairn. The path resumes down to the 'wrought-iron' cairn on Lesser Man, then drops more steeply to rejoin the tourist path as it passes back out of the fence. The fact that a century-old guidebook describes this path as infallible is testament to its popularity and the unlikelihood of going astray! Turn right on this for a straightforward descent all the way with super views, to pass through another fence above Whit Beck before finally levelling out. The path runs past the

Hawell monument (recalling several members of a local shepherding family) and on to a kissing-gate off the fell, then traces a fieldside along to the car park at the terminus of Gale Road.

Turn right through the car park but as the road begins, pass through a kissing-gate on the left onto a bridleway bound directly for Keswick. This is followed unfailingly down the flank of Latrigg, some recent felling having opened out more views. Ignore a branch left up towards Latrigg, and simply remain on this super path all the way. The only point to be careful is after rounding a deep-cut little stream, a wider way bears off left into the plantations: take the right-hand path descending more directly, by gorse and down the side of Latrigg Woods to a gate at the bottom corner.

Pass the house at Spooney Green and cross over the high by-pass bridge on the access road down to Brundholme Road at Briar Rigg. Go briefly right to the old rail bridge site on the edge of Crosthwaite, then take a gate on the left to join a suburban path. Go left beneath the old rail embankment to enter Fitz Park, and follow the path away to join the riverbank leading to the far corner, where Station Road is joined. Cross the bridge to re-enter the centre of town.

Derwentwater and Skiddaw

CALDBECK TO CARLISLE

DISTANCE *14 miles (22¹²km)*

ORDNANCE SURVEY MAPS
1:50,000
Landranger 90 - Penrith, Keswick & Ambleside
Landranger 85 - Carlisle & Solway Firth
1:25,000
Explorer OL5 - English Lakes North East
Explorer 315 - Carlisle

> *This final stage of the Cumbria Way is by far the easiest, so after the ups and downs of Lakeland it's simple country walking, mostly in the faithful company of the lovely River Caldew.*

Leave Caldbeck by crossing the main road bridge north of the pub, and with the car park on your left, turn right along Friar Row. Alternatively, this road can be joined by taking the walled snicket down the near side of the church, to cross an enchanting stone arched foot-bridge on the Cald Beck alongside the well. Either way, head right along the road which quickly terminates at the edge of the village. Ignoring a stile on the left, pass through the gate in front and follow the firm track downstream to quickly expire at the sewage works. Pass round to the right to find a gate into the woodland of Parson's Park.

Head away on the clear path, which quickly turns left to rise away from the beck, climbing through plantations before levelling out. Sections of this can be rather muddy. Ignore a thin, level path through conifers ahead, and continue a slighter rise to meet a level way. Turn right along here on an improved way with scrub above and conifers below. A large felled area opens out below, giving sweeping views over the wooded confluence of Cald Beck with old and soon to be firm friend the Caldew, backed by the pair of wind turbines at Newlands. A contrastingly narrow, firm section slants up to a bridle-gate into open country, at 590ft/180m the high point of this stage. A faint little path contours across terrain made colourful by gorse and bracken. *Hesket Newmarket is revealed across to the right beneath the Caldbeck Fells.*

Passing though a gate just above a wood corner, bear left to the far top corner of the enveloping woodland, where a bridle-gate admits back into the trees. This is effectively your last real look back at the

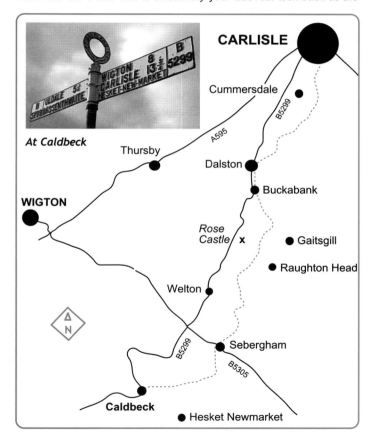

At Caldbeck

fells. A good path heads away, soon arriving at the terminus of a forestry track. This quickly leads to a gate across it: here abandon the impending forest road and slip right onto a contrastingly narrow, firm path slanting down an extensive felled slope. At the bottom the Caldew is joined and the path heads downstream in its company. While the river races enthusiastically over rocky sections, the broad path runs on and through a restored landslip to a gate out of the trees. Bear left along the field edge beneath the wooded bank, a farm track forming at the next gate and becoming firmer still at the next, where another track joins from the left. This leads out by the returning river onto the B5305 Wigton-Penrith road at a shapely bridge below Sebergham.

Cross the bridge and rise a short way up the road before turning left behind a house. Through a small gate a nice little path slants up scrubby ground giving a view over the environs of the bridge. At the top it doubles back right to a bridle-gate to the rear of an imposing red-brick house, and its surfaced access road leads out to reach the church in view ahead. *The tiny village is further on the road, but offers little of interest. The small, early 19th century church of St Mary is entered at the base of the little tower, which also has exterior steps. Just yards further a bell remains in place at the old school.*

Bell Bridge on the River Caldew

Leave the road by turning left through a gate opposite the church gate. An enclosed cart track heads away to approach Sebergham Hall. In front of its immediate grounds the track bears right through a gate, and resumes past the hall to meet its access road at the other side of the farm buildings. Continue on this firmer hedgeside way, enjoying a wide panorama before descending to a minor road at Bell Bridge. Turn left over this very elegant single arch to a road junction. Turn neither way however, but a stile on the right at the bridge-end sees stone steps deposit you on the riverbank. Turn downstream in delightful surrounds to commence a lengthy, unbroken spell in the company of the Caldew.

Apart from an early footbridge on a mill-race just before the old mill it served, simply remain on the bank, encountering several stiles before a park-like section past Bog Bridge, a footbridge. After a bend beyond isolated Holm House on the other bank, note that maps showing the path leaving the bank are out of date: it now faithfully shadows the river all the way to the road at Rose Bridge. En route, a pleasant pencil wood is traversed to emerge into more park-like surrounds.

The buildings of Raughton Head are seen up to the right, while revealed over to the left is imposing Rose Castle. *The official residence of the Bishops of Carlisle for around 700 years, it has seen countless changes down the years. Alongside the big house stands an extremely impressive pele tower, which originates from the early 14th century when fortification against Scots' raids was essential. The house has seen many skirmishes, and suffered much destruction during the Civil War.* Several stiles are encountered before a few steps lead to an old iron kissing-gate onto the road at the three-arched bridge.

Cross the road, not the bridge, and resume as before. The path remains on the bank as far as a bend just short of the start of Willowclose Wood. Here the thin trod slants left towards the left edge of the wood, crossing a tiny footbridge and rising gently to a kissing-gate on the brow. Go straight across this parkland, with Lime House appearing in the trees ahead. The thin path runs to an iron kissing-gate onto a cart track within the grounds. Turn left on this to the front of the house, where the drive is met. Across a neat lawn is this attractive old house which currently operates as a school. Go straight across to a gate from where a splendid old grass way heads across more parkland. Through a gate at the end an access track is joined from the house below. Head up this the short way to a bend of a surfaced access road at Holmhill Farm. Across to your right is a vast sweep of flat parkland.

Turn right on the road to its early demise at Hawksdale Hall, a very elegant Georgian house. From a gate on the right follow a track swinging left across the field. Joining a fence corner it rises gently to a gate, then heads faintly off over a gentle brow, at the end passing into a briefly enclosed section. Emerging at a gate it swings sharp left to join an access road and out onto the B5299 Caldbeck-Dalston road. Turn right down the footway into Bridge End. *At this busy little corner are the Bridge End Inn and a service station alongside Hawksdale Bridge.*

Turn immediately over the sturdy road bridge, and reaching a fork you have a brief choice of routes through suburban Buckabank. The official route forks left to a T-junction alongside another bridge, then sharp right until bridging the mill-stream, where turn left on a parallel access road. Preferably however bear right, and immediately after the old red sandstone Bishops Mill, turn left then sharply right on an access road alongside a mill-stream. Re-united, the Way follows the road to Ellers Mill, where the old millpond sits beneath a tall chimney. Keep straight on through the yard, where the old road continues (note the grand mill-owner's house on the left), rejoined by the mill-stream, to join another road. Turn left on this, bridging the stream to quickly cross the Caldew on White Bridge. *The original bridge of 1899 was rebuilt exactly a century later, and happily today is closed to vehicles.* The old road continues across open ground alongside the green to rejoin the B5299 at Dalston. *Note, on the left at the junction, some neat almshouses of 1815.* Bear right on the main road to the village centre.

Dalston is a pleasant spot focused around a busy little square. Gathered around are the Blue Bell Inn, a Post office, several shops, a cafe and a bakery. Restored in 1890, the sandstone church of St Michael stands at one side, while just north of the village is Dalston Hall, which incorporates a 15th-century pele tower. Dalston is the first station out of Carlisle on the Cumbrian Coast line, and wouldn't be the worst place to end your walk if the need arose. Indeed it would be ideal should the riverbank flood, as can happen on this final section after heavy rain (flooding totally devastated Carlisle in January 2005). However, the Caldew beckons again, and despite odd reservations, it does lead rather cleverly all the way to the finish. Keep straight on the road past the church, and immediately after the primary school an enclosed path turns sharp right. Since the turn of the Millennium the route hereafter has been transformed into the Caldew Cycleway, which effectively over-rides the Cumbria Way all the way into Carlisle.

The trail joins the riverbank and turns left between Caldew School sports fields and the Caldew itself. *The inevitable hard surface makes a grand cycle route, though as the walkers that were here first, most of us would prefer a more traditional path underfoot.* Beyond the school fields a large factory is passed, and more open surrounds lead near the sewage works before forging on to become enclosed by railway and river. Judging by several warning signs the greatest threat in these parts is that of damp, as you must beware sprinklers as well as flooding. Remain on this infallible way close by the railway, and as the river returns, the railway bridges it at the former Cummersdale station. *Anyone over eight feet tall must heed the warning 'low bridge', the rest of us should manage to squeeze under unharmed.* A little further the way meets a bend on the surfaced Caldew Road. *If desperate, this climbs left into Cummersdale, which has a pub, the Spinners Arms.*

Continue on the riverside road to its demise at a factory entrance. Ignoring a metal footbridge, the path squeezes between the extensive factory and the river. At the end of the factory fence, a fork gives an escape from the unrelenting trail. While the cycleway rises slightly left, a stile on the right sends a footpath through nicer riverside greenery. This short spell ends at a stile. Though a path runs left to the cycleway, the footpath passes through a kissing-gate to resume on the open riverbank. The outskirts of Carlisle are now just ahead. The path remains on the riverbank, approaching housing ahead and entering dog-walkers' territory. Through a gate the surfaced way rejoins from the left at Denton Holme. Resume on a roadway past a former mill, a weir and a pub to reach a metal footbridge on the river. Ignore this and continue on the surfaced path (the Caldew Riverside Trail) past sports fields to an identical bridge. Again ignore and forge on past old buildings to an impasse, where turn left along terraced Metcalfe Street. At the end turn right on busy Denton Street. There are two concluding options.

• The direct route remains on Denton Street into town, bridging the river, going straight across on the road over the Victoria Viaduct of 1877 to reach English Street, where turn left to enter Green Market. In front of the old Town Hall stands Carlisle (Carel) Cross, which dates from 1682 and marks the official finish.

• The longer route turns right off Denton Street along Thomas Street, then left on Lime Street to rejoin the river. The trail traces an old railway beneath Nelson Bridge before bridging the Caldew for the last time, following its east bank to emerge onto Viaduct Estate Road.

Go left and up onto Bridge Street at the end, then right. Over to the left stands the castle, while you turn right on Abbey Street, swinging left in front of the cathedral along Paternoster Row onto Castle Street. Turn right to finish in pedestrianised Green Market. In front of the Tourist Information Centre in the old Town Hall stands Carlisle (Carel) Cross which dates from 1682, and it marks the official finish. Well done!

Carlisle is the administrative centre for Cumbria, and has been a Border stronghold for many centuries. Such is its isolation in the north-west that the nearest larger centre is Newcastle, on the east coast! Its numerous buildings of note all glow with the red sandstone of the Eden Valley, and it is through the city that the county's major river flows to enter the Solway Firth: Carlisle also overlooks the Caldew's confluence with the Eden. Strategically built above this confluence is the hugely impressive red sandstone Carlisle Castle, which dates from 1092 and has seen much warfare and trouble down the centuries. The tall keep commands spectacularly extensive views from the Lakeland Fells across to the North Pennines, and north across the Solway into Scotland. This is also home to the King's Own Royal Border Regiment and their museum is on the site. It is in the care of English Heritage.

Of equal historical and present significance is Carlisle Cathedral, founded in 1122 and an impressive delight. Of particular note are the East Window containing 14th century glass, the vaulted, painted ceiling of the Choir and a 16th century carved Flemish altarpiece in St Wilfrid's Chapel. Note also a visitor centre in the Fratry, and the Prior's Tower Museum. Medieval town walls have survived on the western side of the city above the Caldew, while the Tullie House Museum offers an absorbing insight into the area's colourful past. Carlisle also presides over the western reaches of Hadrian's Wall, and Stanwix fort on the north bank of the Eden was the largest on the frontier, holding 1000 men and horses.

The Cross, Carlisle

A FELLWALK FROM CALDBECK

DISTANCE 11^{1}2 miles / 18^{1}2km   *ASCENT 2445ft / 745m*

SUMMITS
Brae Fell	*1922ft / 685*	*Great Sca Fell*	*2135ft / 651m*
Knott	*2329ft / 710m*	*High Pike*	*2159ft / 658m*

ORDNANCE SURVEY MAPS
1:50,000 - Landranger 90
1:25,000 - Explorer OL4 & Explorer OL5

Leave the village by heading west on the B5299 Uldale road. On climbing to the school on the edge of the village, take the unsigned lane to the left. Keep right at a fork to rise to run on to a T-junction at Wath. Turn right, soon commencing a steep climb past a big old limekiln before levelling out. At a junction take the left turn, rising again to run on to approach the hamlet of Fell Side.

Take a walled lane on the left before the first building, an outdoor centre. This soon reaches a gate onto the fell. Take the concrete track rising away, but quickly leave it as the intake wall drops away, instead bear right on a grassy way contouring right to meet a clearer way to rejoin the intake wall on the right, above a cottage. Just yards further you join a hard track which has just gained the open fell, this is the old Roughton Gill mine road. Resume along this, rising then running on to reveal the colourful enclave of Roughton Gill itself just ahead. *Lead and copper were mined in this once busy, now tranquil location. Already you can enjoy a massive panorama out to the north.* After the wall drops away, look across the valley to see a quad track scaling the grassy slopes of Brae Fell, rising directly to the summit cairn. At once you can drop off the mine road on a grassy track slanting down to merge with one from a little further along to reach a ford on Dale Beck. There is a risk of wet feet after rain, but it is normally problem-free.

Across, an inviting grass track begins the simple ascent. *Views into Roughton Gill are replaced by a wider prospect out to the distinctive 1868ft/569m Criffel across the Solway Firth.* Keep right on the more obvious ascending way at a fork, passing a trio of pools on a shelf and continuing up to suddenly reveal the cairn just ahead. *Brae Fell boasts a fine cairn, and its view is equally impressive. This ranges from the might of nearby Skiddaw, over the lower reach of Bassenthwaite Lake and little Over Water, out to an extensive panorama over the Solway Firth and North Cumbria.*

Resume on the obvious path heading south along the connecting ridge, down to a slight dip and immediately forking as you start to rise. Take the right branch which slants up to gain the waiting cairn on Little Sca Fell, alongside a small hollow. Again a path resumes, through another slight drop before a steep little pull onto neighbouring Great Sca Fell. *This flatter top has a less inspiring cairn, now looking to the waiting bulk of Knott.* The last dip before the walk's high point sees you crossing the edge of a peaty area before a steady rise up the great dome of Knott, easing out to cross more faintly to the scrappy cairn doing ill service to this patriarch of the Uldale Fells.

Knott is the kingpin of the great mass of open country north of Skiddaw Forest, with broad shoulders emanating in every direction. A clear day is essential for a viewpoint whose redemption is found in its distant panorama: the Solway Firth appears as at one's feet, with old favourite Criffel upstaged by a fine array of Galloway Hills. This is just a sample of the rich fare provided in a northern arc stretching from the Isle of Man to Cross Fell. Looking south into Lakeland, there is a glimpse of Thirlmere through the Blencathra-Lonscale Fell gap.

Rather handily you can also pick out the Lingy Hut to the north-east, a mile distant as the crow flies, but rather longer by the best route: this is your next objective en route to High Pike, by which time you will have merged with the Cumbria Way. Leave by heading east, the path forming within a few paces to head down and then along Knott's broad eastern shoulder. After a good half-mile the way swings left well before the end of the shoulder, the path dropping more emphatically to the marshy edge of Miller Moss. Cross the tiny stream of Grains Gill draining the moss, and head away on a quickly improving path running to the waiting Lingy Hut.

The former shooters' cabin of Lingy Hut is a useful shelter from the elements, and is maintained as a bothy by the National Park Authority. A visitors book gives evidence of its popularity. You are by now on the Cumbria Way all the way back to Caldbeck, so if you don't already know it, you can pick up the route description from the Lingy Hut at the top of page 58.

USEFUL ADDRESSES

Ramblers' Association
2nd Floor, Camelford House, 87-89 Albert Embankment, London SE1 7BR
• 020-7339 8500

Lake District National Park Visitor Services
Brockhole, Windermere, Cumbria LA23 1LJ
• 015394-46601

Information Centres

Coronation Hall, County Square **Ulverston** LA12 7LZ • 01229-587120

Ruskin Avenue **Coniston** LA21 8EH • 015394-41533

Central Buildings, Market Cross **Ambleside** LA22 9BS • 015394-32582

Seatoller Barn **Seatoller** Keswick CA12 5XN • 017687-77294

Moot Hall, Market Square **Keswick** CA12 5JR • 017687-72645

Old Town Hall, Green Market **Carlisle** CA3 8JD • 01228-625600

Cumbria Tourist Board
Ashleigh, Holly Road, Windermere LA23 2AQ
• 015394-44444

The National Trust North West Regional Office
The Hollens, Grasmere, Ambleside, Cumbria LA22 9QZ
• 0870-609 5391

Friends of the Lake District
Murley Moss, Kendal, Cumbria LA9 7SS
• 01539-720788

Public Transport Information
Traveline • 0870 608 2608
National Rail Enquiries • 08457-484950

Lake District National Park Weatherline
• 017687-75757

INDEX

Principal features on the Cumbria Way (illustrations in italic)

Carlisle Castle

WALK LOG

Date	Place	Miles daily	Miles total	Notes
	Ulverston	-	-	
	Broughton Beck	$3\frac{1}{2}$	$3\frac{1}{2}$	
	Gawthwaite	5	5	
	Beacon Tarn	9	9	
	Coniston Water	12	12	
	Coniston	$15\frac{1}{2}$	$15\frac{1}{2}$	
	Tarn Hows	$2\frac{1}{2}$	18	
	High Park	6	$21\frac{1}{2}$	
	Skelwith Bridge	$7\frac{1}{2}$	23	
	Elterwater	$9\frac{1}{4}$	$24\frac{3}{4}$	
	Chapel Stile	10	$25\frac{1}{2}$	
	Old Dungeon Ghyll	$12\frac{1}{2}$	28	
	Stake Pass	3	31	
	Stonethwaite	$6\frac{3}{4}$	$34\frac{3}{4}$	
	Rosthwaite	$7\frac{3}{4}$	$35\frac{3}{4}$	
	Grange	$9\frac{3}{4}$	$37\frac{3}{4}$	
	Hawse End	$12\frac{1}{2}$	$40\frac{1}{2}$	
	Portinscale	14	42	
	Keswick	15	43	
	Latrigg car park	$1\frac{3}{4}$	$44\frac{3}{4}$	
	Skiddaw House	$5\frac{1}{4}$	$48\frac{1}{4}$	
	Carrock Mine road	9	52	
	Lingy Hut	$10\frac{1}{2}$	$53\frac{1}{2}$	
	High Pike	$11\frac{1}{2}$	$54\frac{1}{2}$	
	Nether Row	$13\frac{1}{2}$	$56\frac{1}{2}$	
	Caldbeck	15	58	
	Sebergham	$3\frac{1}{2}$	$61\frac{1}{2}$	
	Rose Bridge	$6\frac{3}{4}$	$64\frac{3}{4}$	
	Bridge End	$8\frac{3}{4}$	$66\frac{3}{4}$	
	Dalston	$9\frac{3}{4}$	$67\frac{3}{4}$	
	Cummersdale	12	70	
	Carlisle	14	72	